DATA FLOW COMPUTING

ELLIS HORWOOD SERIES IN COMPUTERS AND THEIR APPLICATIONS

Series Editor: Brian Meek, Director of the Computer Unit, Queen Elizabeth College, University of London

DATA FLOW COMPUTING

J. A. SHARP, B.Sc., Ph.D.
Lecturer in Computer Science
Department of Mathematics and Computer Science
University College of Swansea, Wales

ELLIS HORWOOD LIMITED
Publishers · Chichester

Halsted Press: a division of
JOHN WILEY & SONS
New York · Chichester · Brisbane · Toronto

First published in 1985 by

ELLIS HORWOOD LIMITED
Market Cross House, Cooper Street, Chichester, West Sussex, PO19 1EB, England

The publisher's colophon is reproduced from James Gillison's drawing of the ancient Market Cross, Chichester.

Distributors:

Australia, New Zealand, South-east Asia:
Jacaranda-Wiley Ltd., Jacaranda Press,
JOHN WILEY & SONS INC.,
G.P.O. Box 859, Brisbane, Queensland 40001, Australia

Canada:
JOHN WILEY & SONS CANADA LIMITED
22 Worcester Road, Rexdale, Ontario, Canada.

Europe, Africa:
JOHN WILEY & SONS LIMITED
Baffins Lane, Chichester, West Sussex, England.

North and South America and the rest of the world:
Halsted Press: a division of
JOHN WILEY & SONS
605 Third Avenue, New York, N.Y. 10016, U.S.A.

© 1985 J.A. Sharp/Ellis Horwood Limited

British Library Cataloguing in Publication Data
Sharp, J.A.
Data flow computing. —
(Ellis Horwood series in computers and their applications)
1. Electronic digital computers — Programming
I. Title
001.64'2   QA76.6
Library of Congress Card No. 84-28957
ISBN 0-85312-724-7 (Ellis Horwood Limited)
ISBN 0-470-20167-3 (Halsted Press)
Typeset by Ellis Horwood Limited
Printed in Great Britain by R.J. Acford, Chichester

Table of Contents

To my wife Pam
and our son Richard

Prologue

In the past few years there has been an increasing interest in data flow programming techniques. This interest has been motivated partly by the rapid advances in technology (and the need for distributed processing techniques), partly by a desire for faster throughput by applying parallel processing techniques, and partly by a search for a programming tool that is closer to the problem-solving methods which people naturally adopt than current programming languages. Current languages are often referred to as problem-oriented, but their design has been strongly influenced by the design of the computers that they are used with and thus they are still to a certain extent machine-oriented. How the approach discussed in this book allows us to develop languages that are not machine-oriented should become clearer later. The languages we discuss will, of course, be biased towards a particular method of problem solving, but this will be a machine-independent method.

The data flow approach is often associated solely with the use of data-driven computations. In this book both data-driven and demand-driven computations will be taken as being valid forms of data flow computations. The differences between the two alternative approaches will be discussed in a later chapter.

With the advent of the microprocessor and the ever-advancing technology of integrated circuits it is becoming increasingly obvious that we need to break away from the straitjacket of the conventional approach to computing. The principles upon which it has been based are becoming less and less realistic in the light of present-day knowledge. One obvious illustration of the inadequacy of the conventional approach is the way in which millions of memory cells are associated with only one processor. The same technology is used to develop both processors and memory circuits, yet the processor is being efficiently utilised and is in constant use, whereas memory cells are sitting idle for most of the time, and being grossly under-utilized. We are not proposing that we should use memory cells merely to increase some theoretical utilization measure, but rather indicating that there is clearly a possibility that by using the memory available more efficiently we may be able either to run programs faster or to execute larger programs with the same resources.

Although there have been earlier attempts to break away from the traditional approach, none have been totally successful in achieving popular support and also they have nearly always assumed that any language implementation would be based on a single sequential processor.

The so-called software crisis has led many eminent computer scientists to call for a more structured approach to the design of programs. This is another reason for us to rethink our whole approach to programming in the light of current technology.

The data flow approach discussed in this book is an approach which provides an attractive alternative for the solution of the above problems.

The book is divided into four parts. Part I discusses the ways in which computations can be modelled. In order to understand fully the implications of the data flow approach we have to be sure we understand what is meant by the traditional, control flow approach. In this section of the book we also introduce the 'functional' or 'applicative' approach to computing which has recently gained much favour, and show how it relates to the data flow approach.

Part II of the book builds on the formal model of computing introduced in the first section, and discusses the implications for programming languages. The data flow approach is so fundamentally different from that usually adopted that new programming notations have to be introduced.

We next turn to the implementation of the data flow model of computing, and the various concepts necessary are discussed in Part III. A variety of data flow machine architectures have been proposed, and these are discussed in Chapter 15.

The final section of the book discusses how the data flow programming languages proposed could be implemented on the new machine architectures suggested in Part III. In addition we consider how the basic notion of a machine is extended to that of a computer system which can be used in a realistic context.

This book presents the author's own personal view of the data flow approach to computing. Other researchers are likely to have a different perspective. A brief survey of some of the work done by various people in related areas is included at the end of the book. The author offers his apologies in advance to anyone who feels that their contributions to the subject have been either misrepresented or omitted, and trusts that they will accept this book as it was intended — as one individual's view of data flow and not as a definitive text.

Acknowledgements

I would like to thank all my colleagues, in particular the members of the Westfield College Distributed Processing Research Group, who have indirectly contributed to the contents of this book both by presenting their own ideas and by discussing my work.

I thank the authors for permission to use an extract from 'A case study in disciplined design' in Infotech State of the Art Report on Structured Programming by L. Presser and C. Rector (Pergamon Infotech Ltd., 1976), and also Recursive Programming Techniques by W. H. Burge (Addison-Wesley, 1975).

Finally, I would like to thank Michael Horwood for suggesting that this book might be written, and 'the man with the red pen' for helping the project reach fruition.

Part

I

MODELS OF COMPUTING

1

Introduction

In order to do anything useful with a computer system we must be able to specify what operations we want to be carried out. This usually implies that a program needs to be written. Exceptions to this are dedicated systems that are designed to implement a limited range of functions. Even then the designer of the system has had to specify a form of program for the system to execute, either permanently stored in memory, or 'hard-wired' into the control circuitry of the machine itself.

In specifying the operations to be done we make assumptions about what primitive operations are available, and also about how they are carried out. In other words we have in mind a picture of how the computations we are specifying will be executed. This picture of how things are done is referred to as a model of computing. Programmers are not always aware that this is what they are doing since any programming language automatically provides us with a model of computing. This model may be an abstraction of the physical processes involved in the operation of computer hardware. Conventional programming languages nearly all assume the existence of a primitive set of arithmetic operations (add, multiply etc.). They also assume that these operations are carried out sequentially on data stored in some form of memory device. Alternatively the model may be a more formal one, developed using mathematical theory, which is totally independent of hardware operations. Lisp uses a formal model of computing that is less hardware dependent but still assumes that it will be implemented on a traditional digital computer.

Most existing programming languages were designed for use on computers based on John von Neumann's original concept. This is why they implicitly take as their model of computing the traditional execution cycle (fetch; execute; store) proposed by von Neumann, and adopted in virtually all digital computers since. This model of computing is referred to both as the von Neumann model and as the control flow model.

The aim of this first part of the book is to discuss various alternative models of computing that have been developed and, in particular, to introduce the model of computing known as the data flow model. In order to do so it is necessary first to review our understanding of the traditional control flow model that we are all used to, and in Chapter 2 we will discuss in more detail how the traditional approach to computing is influenced by the structure of the von Neumann computer. The data flow approach is then presented in Chapter 3, and a closely related approach to computing − namely the functional approach − is the subject discussed in Chapter 4.

Firstly, though, let us introduce some terminology that will aid our discussion of models of computing. Some of the definitions given will be rather imprecise, relying upon some intuitive ideas that have yet to be defined formally; but we shall return to them in later chapters, when we will be in a position to make them rather more precise.

We define a **program** as the specification of a set of operations that are required in order to carry out some task. No formal definition of an operation will be given for the moment. Suffice it to say that examples are conventional machine operations (such as add, subtract etc.).

Two aspects of this definition of a program should be emphasised.

(a) No ordering of the operations is implied.
(b) Not all operations will be executed for all sets of input data.

The subset of operations that are executed given a particular set of input data defines a **computation**.

Two ordering conventions will now be defined. The **control flow** ordering is based on the idea of a temporal sequence of operations. The **data flow** ordering, on the other hand, is based on the need for data.

− A **data flow program** is one in which the ordering of operations is not specified by the programmer, but is that implied by the data interdependencies.

— A **control flow program** is one in which there is a total ordering of operations specified by the programmer.

Hence:

— A **data flow computation** is one in which the operations are executed in an order determined by the data interdependencies and the availability of resources.
— A **control flow computation** is one in which the operations are executed in an order predetermined by a control convention, used by the programmer.

Two varieties of data flow computation can be distinguished:

(a) **data-driven computations** in which operations are executed in an order determined by the availability of input data;
(b) **demand-driven computations** in which operations are executed in an order determined by the requirements for data.

The data flow approach is often associated solely with the use of data-driven computations. In this book both data-driven and demand-driven computations will be taken as being valid forms of data flow computation. The differences between the two alternative approaches will be discussed in later chapters.

2

The control flow approach

Most people who have done any computing have an intuitive notion of what is meant by a von Neumann computer. We refer, of course, to the design formulated by researchers (including John von Neumann) just after the Second World War, in which the program is held in memory and a single sequence control register points at one instruction after another causing the execution of the instruction currently being pointed at [GvN63].

The basic design is shown in Fig. 2.1 and consists of five components:

- an input unit
- an output unit
- a memory unit
- an arithmetic and logic computation unit (ALU)
- a control unit

To perform a computation two overlapping cycles of steps are performed:

The instruction cycle
- the address of the next instruction is transferred from the program counter or sequence control register (SCR) in the control unit to the memory unit;
- a read command is sent from the control unit to the memory unit causing the appropriate instruction to be read from the memory unit;

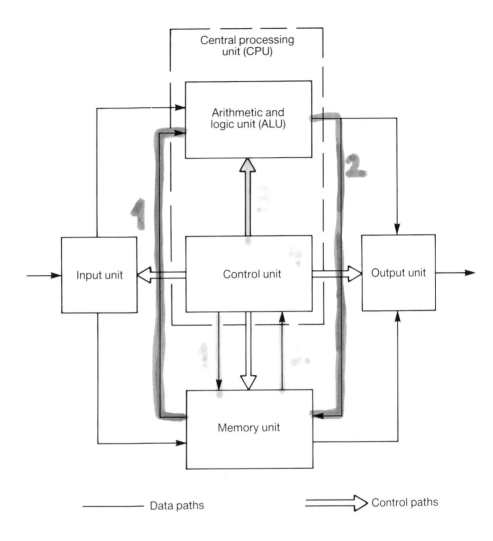

Fig. 2.1 — Block diagram of typical von Neumann computer.

— the op-code part of the instruction is transferred to the control
unit;
— this is then decoded and the appropriate signals are sent from the
control unit to the ALU;
— the contents of the SCR are set to the address of the next instruction.

Overlapping with the penultimate phase of the above cycle we have:

The execution cycle

— if data is required from the memory unit the control unit sends the appropriate command and data is transferred from the memory unit to the ALU;

— the ALU carries out the operation required;

— if data is to be stored in the memory unit the control unit issues the appropriate command and data is transferred from the ALU to the memory unit.

Much of the time taken for execution is taken up by the transfer of information from one component of the machine to another. In traditional programming languages this mode of operation is mirrored by the existence of the assignment statement, and the existence of variables. The assignment operation represents the transfer of results from the ALU to the memory unit. Every reference to a variable (other than on the left-hand side of an assignment) represents the transfer of data to the ALU from the memory unit. Conventional languages are built up from the primitive notions of storing data in variables (memory locations), taking these values, operating upon them, and assigning the result back to another variable.

The existence of the SCR is mirrored in conventional high-level languages by the existence of specific control instructions such as **goto**, conditional statements, and loops. All control constructs work by altering the order in which statements are executed. That is, instead of just incrementing the SCR a new value is assigned to it so that rather than the next instruction in sequence being carried out control passes to another part of the program. Thus it is possible to regard control constructs as special forms of assignment instructions that make assignments to the SCR. Procedure calls are rather different in that, although an assignment is made to the SCR in order to execute the procedure, which is presumably stored in another part of the memory, the existing value of the SCR must be remembered in order to allow the procedure to return control back to the calling instruction.

With operations being performed in a strict sequence a computation consists of a sequence of well-separated events. This means that the concept of the state of a computation is meaningful. The state may be represented by the contents of the SCR and the memory after each instruction/execution cycle. Also the concept of a programming variable, which may change its value as the state changes, is a concept that is only meaningful because of the sequential nature of the model.

Let us now recall the definition of control flow programs, and computations given in the introduction.

— a **control flow program** is one in which there is a total ordering of the operations specified by the programmer.

— a **control flow computation** is one in which operations are executed in an order predetermined by a control convention, used by the programmer.

It is easy to see how the traditional von Neumann model of computing implies that programs and computations must take the above form. The next instruction to be performed, or to be carried out, is determined by the contents of the SCR. Statements are assumed to be executed sequentially unless specific assignments are made to the SCR using explicit control structures. Thus the programmer is totally responsible for specifying the order of execution. The only alternative is to propose some other means of controlling the contents of the SCR.

This does not mean that it is impossible to introduce some form of parallel execution into the control flow model of computing. Let us now consider how this might be done. Clearly we need to model the idea of operations being carried out concurrently, so the obvious approach would be to introduce the idea of parallel flow of control. This could be implemented using multiple SCRs. By implication we then either need to duplicate control and execution units in order to achieve true simultaneous execution, or we need some mechanism whereby a single set of control and execution units might operate concurrently. We may define a **processor** as a set of control and execution units that can perform a series of execution/instruction cycles independently. A processor may be a physically distinct piece of hardware or, more likely in present-day machines, we have the concept of an **abstract processor** which may or may not be mapped onto a single physical processor. One example of the way such an approach is mirrored in a programming language is the use of **fork** and **join** instructions in Anderson's work [And65]. Consider the following program (which is not written in any particular language) to calculate the roots of a quadratic equation ($ax^2 + bx + c$).

```
begin  input (a, b, c);
       a := 2 * a;
       c := b↑2 − 2 * a * c;
       c := sqrt(c);
       c := c / a;
       b := − b / a;
       a := b + c;
       b := b − c;
       output (a, b)
end
```

In order to exploit the maximum amount of parallelism in this simple program using fork and join constructs, we would need to write:

```
begin input (a, b, c);
      a := 2 * a;
      c := b↑2 − 2 * a * c;
      fork L1, L2;              {control passes to labels L1
                                 and L2; those blocks are
                                 executed in parallel}
  L1: begin c := sqrt(c);
            c := c / a;
            goto L3
      end;
  L2: begin b := − b / a;
            goto L3
      end;
  L3: join L1, L2;             {wait until both the preced-
                                ing blocks have finished}
      fork L4, L5;             {perform the blocks L4 and
                                L5 in parallel}
  L4: begin a := b + c;
            goto L6
      end;
  L5: begin b := b − c;
            goto L6
      end;
  L6: join L4, L5;             {wait until both L4 and L5
                                are done}

      output (a, b)
end
```

With this approach the amount of control information that needs to be specified obviously soon begins to obscure the details of the actual program. A neater notation can be devised. The collateral clauses of Algol 68 could be used (possibly with extensions), but this does not change the fact that the programmer still has to discover, and specify, all the parallel control structure. It seems rather unattractive to base a language on a model which assumes the existence of a number of processors that is unlikely to be the same as the number of processors in the actual machine − unless, that is, we are separating the concept of actual processors from the abstract concept of 'processors', by allowing one physical processor to execute two or more processes concurrently in a form of pseudo-parallelism.

Another possible approach to the introduction of parallelism into the control flow approach is the idea of communicating sequential processes.

Here we need to define the concept of a process. A **process** is a subset of the operations in a program that may be performed sequentially.

With this approach a set of parallel sequential processes is envisaged, which send and receive data items to and from the other processes. Thus a short sequential program needs to be written for each process, and communication instructions such as 'send' and 'receive' are required. The version of the quadratic roots program presented below does not use any published notation, but should serve as an example. Hoare's model [Hoa78] uses the same fundamental concept of communicating sequential processes, but the notation he uses allows for the construction of more generalised abstract processes at a lower level.

In the following example variable names are global to both processes, and thus there is no need to introduce additional port names.

```
begin process one :
      begin  input (a, b, c)
             send (b);              {the value of the variable b
                                     is sent to the other process}

             a := 2 * a;
             send (a);              {the same for a}
             c := b↑2 − 2 * a * c;
             c := sqrt(c);
             c := c / a;
             send(c);               {and for c}
             receive(b1);           {a value labelled b1 is sent
                                     by the other process; com-
                                     putation cannot proceed
                                     until this value is received}

             a := b1 + c;
             receive(d);            {similarly for a value d}
             output(a, d)
      end;
```

```
      process two :
      begin receive(b);              {process two waits to receive
                                      a value from process one
                                      before it can start}

            receive(a);              {it then accepts a second
                                      value}

            b1 := − b / a;
            send(b1);                {sends one to process one}
            receive(c);              {receives another}
            d := b1 − c;
            send(d)                  {and finally sends the value
                                      of d to process one}
      end
end
```

The assumption upon which this approach works is that each abstract process is executed on a single processor (abstract or physical). Once again we have the unattractive prospect of the number of processors assumed in the model being different from the number of actual processors. Also the amount of control information that needs to be specified seems to be excessive.

These problems occur because the model still emphasises the notion of control. Parallel control can only be introduced after studying the operations which act upon the data, and by seeing which may be performed in parallel. A change in emphasis is required, if we are to avoid this rather burdensome task. In the data-oriented model, which is introduced in the next chapter, it is shown how, by adopting a different model of computing which does not mirror the structure of the von Neumann computer so closely, we can relieve the programmer of the burden of detecting and specifying all the possible parallelism.

3

The data flow approach

The data flow model of computing attempts to get round the problems encountered in introducing parallelism into the traditional control flow model, by looking at the process of computation from a different viewpoint.

Let us recall the definitions given in Chapter 1.

— A **data flow program** is one in which the ordering of operations is not explicitly specified by the programmer, but is that implied by the data interdependencies.
— A **data flow computation** is one in which operations are executed in an order determined by the data interdependencies and the availability of resources.

It is convenient for the moment to ignore the question of resource availability. This topic might more appropriately be considered to be the province of the implementor of a data flow computing system.

Returning to the quadratic roots example, Fig. 3.1 illustrates graphically the data dependencies between operations (statements). An arrow (→) may be read as 'must be followed by'.

Any model of computing should, ideally, be applicable at all levels. If we take as primitive such operations as add, multiply, etc., we can represent the previous example in a purely graphical manner (see Fig. 3.2).

Of course theoretically we can use much simpler primitives; a logical nand or nor would be sufficient, as we will see in the next chapter.

Before continuing it is important to define more precisely the intuitive notions of program and computation, and ensure that we separate them from the von Neumann ideas of control. A program is often associated with the concept of an algorithm. An **algorithm** specifies a sequence of steps which must be carried out in order to solve a certain problem.

The idea of sequence seems inherent in the notion of an algorithm. So 'algorithm' is synonymous with 'control flow program'.

To separate the notion of program from the notion of algorithm we introduce the following definition, as an extension of that given in Chapter 1.

— A **program** specifies a set of operations (essentially unordered) which must be carried out (in an appropriate order if need be), on a set of input data, in order to produce the desired set of output data.

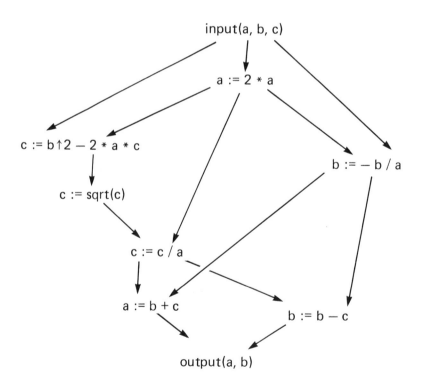

Fig. 3.1 — Data dependencies in a program to find the roots of a quadratic equation.

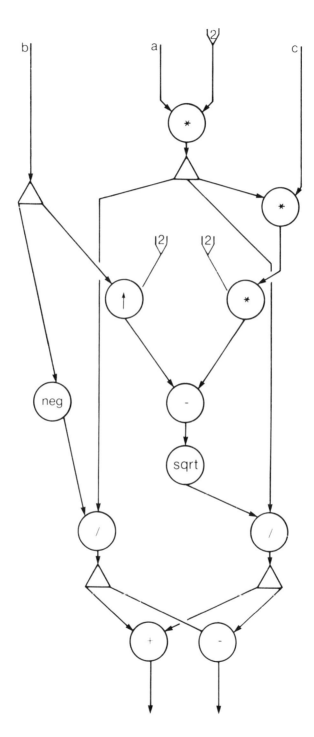

Fig. 3.2 — Primitive operation level data dependencies for a program to find the roots of a quadratic equation.

We have now separated out the idea of sequence from the set of necessary operations; an algorithm is a totally ordered set; a program is a totally unordered set. Clearly some ordering must be imposed upon the set of operations specified in a program since the inputs for some may be the outputs of others. The necessary ordering is, however, only a partial ordering which can be defined by the data interdependencies. What we mean by an operation will become clearer when we present a rather more formal model in Chapter 4.

Thus a data flow program is a program with a partial ordering defined by the data interdependencies, and a control flow program is a program with a total ordering.

When a program is associated with a specific input set, a **computation** is performed and a result produced. The **history** of a computation is the set of operations performed and a record of the order in which they were performed. In this book we shall often refer to a computation as meaning the set of operations performed (or necessary to be performed), and their partial ordering (as defined by the data interdependencies).

It is possible to introduce the idea of a **parallel algorithm** in which certain subsets of the set of operations which make up the program may explicitly be performed in parallel. Thus it is possible using the control flow model to present a parallel algorithm which is equivalent to a data flow program by specifying the order of operations as the same as that implied by the data interdependencies. As we saw in the previous chapter, however, the amount of control information that needs to be specified if we follow this approach seems to be excessive. Another problem associated with this control flow approach is the great variety of orderings that may be possible in a program depending upon the input values.

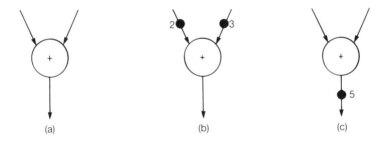

Fig. 3.3 — A simple add node in Rumbaugh's notation. (a) The basic node as used in a data flow schema. (b) The node with data tokens on its input arcs. (c) The node, after firing, with data token on its output arc.

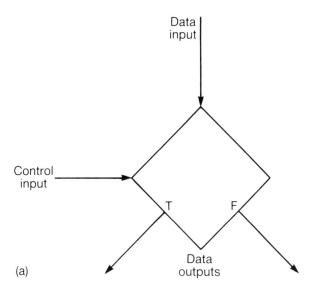

(a)

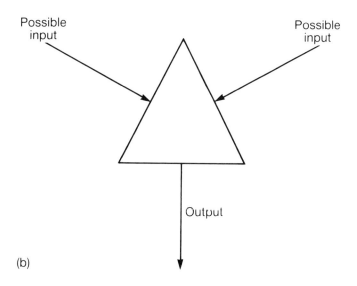

(b)

Fig. 3.4 — Rumbaugh's control nodes. (a) The switch. The input token
is placed on the output arc selected by the control input. (b) The merge.
It is the programmer's responsibility to ensure that only one input
arrives at any one time. The input is then placed on the output.

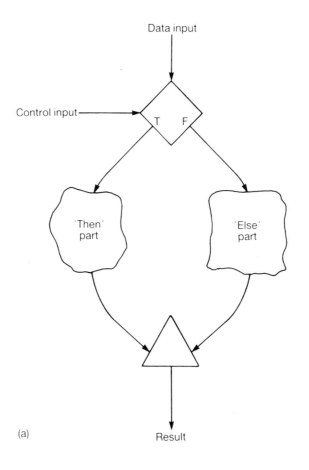

(a)

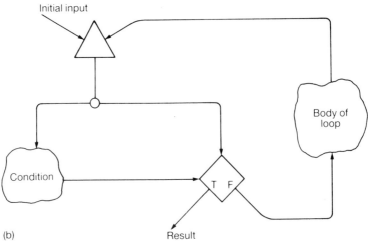

(b)

Fig. 3.5 — Data flow graphs representing typical program constructs.
(a) Conditional. (b) While loop.

A program will normally allow for many possible values of the input data, whereas a computation is associated with only one set of input values. In this sense a program specifies a family of computations.

The usual data flow model of computation is perhaps best illustrated by briefly discussing the work done at MIT by Jack Dennis and others (see [DeJ74], [Rum77]). This approach may be regarded as an example of the classic, data-driven, data flow model. Data flow research started around 1970 with one of the first papers being by Adams [Ada70]. This paper is based on Adams's doctoral thesis that was published in 1968.

The usual data flow model of computing is based on a graphical notation for programs with nodes representing operations and arcs representing data dependencies. We will introduce this idea using Rumbaugh's notation. As an example consider the simple add node in Fig. 3.3. The flow of data along the arcs between the nodes is represented by tokens. Each token represents one data or control value. A control value is in fact only a boolean data value. Only one token may reside upon an arc at any one time. Nodes are said to be **enabled** when there is a token present on all their input arcs (except in the special case of the merge node given later), and no nodes on their output arcs. Any enabled node may **fire** by absorbing the tokens on the input arcs, and placing appropriate tokens on the output arcs.

The nodes available include the standard arithmetic operations such as add, subtract, multiply, divide, etc.

We also need some extra nodes in order to provide some method of making run-time data-dependent decisions as to what operations are to be carried out (see Fig. 3.4).

Conditional and loop graphs may now be constructed as shown in Fig. 3.5. Three points should be noted about this classical model.

(a) Cyclic graphs are allowed.
(b) Multiple tokens may be passed between operations.
(c) Execution is data-driven.

The above graphical notation provides a model of computing by specifying how operations may be combined in order to construct more complex operations. It also makes some assumptions about how the operations are performed (the firing rules).

4

The functional approach

In the previous chapter we presented a graphical model of computation which used the availability of data to drive the execution of a program. In this chapter we shall present a functional definition of the data flow model.

A program defines a mapping from an input domain to an output range. Our earlier discussion assumed the existence of operations that perform such mappings, albeit at a lower level. To formalise our data flow model we have to make the concept of an operation more explicit. In a theoretical sense it is pleasing to make the basis of a model as simple and as primitive as possible. To this end we shall follow convention and define a basic boolean domain for our operations.

$$B = \{TRUE, FALSE\}$$

We could equally well have defined a binary domain,

$$Bi = \{0, 1\}$$

but initially the logical representation seems to add clarity. Later we shall refer to a basic binary domain, and with this in mind we note the equivalence, $B \equiv Bi$.

Conventional logic tells us that the only primitive operation we require is *nor* (or *nand*) (see, for example, [Kor66]).

The primitive operation: *nor*

This operation is defined by a function B × B → B as follows:

$$nor = [a : TRUE , b : B \qquad] FALSE,$$
$$nor = [a : FALSE, b : FALSE] TRUE ,$$
$$nor = [a : FALSE, b : TRUE] FALSE$$

We shall term this method of defining functions as 'definition by cases'. The method of 'definition by cases' is the main definition mechanism provided in this functional data flow model. It may be summarised as shown below.

⟨name of function⟩ = [⟨parameter⟩ : ⟨domain⟩] ⟨value (or expression
                      (repeated for each of   giving value in
                      parameters)   this case)⟩

The only other mechanism, 'definition by composition', is introduced later.

A constant generator

The only other basic operation we need is a constant generator. We shall take as primitive a true generator. This operation requires no input parameter so we introduce the null set {NULL} as a possible domain.

true is defined by a function NULL → TRUE as below,

$$true = [\;] TRUE$$

(a *false* generator could be defined in two ways:

Either *false* = [ ] FALSE,
or *false* = [ ] *nor (true, true)*
)

A copy operation

In combinational logic this operation is usually assumed, and it is not essential if we are allowed to specify the format of the input in a suitable manner. (i.e. by repeating input values to avoid copying.)

copy is defined by a function B → B × B as below:

$$copy = [a : B] (a, a)$$

Complex operations

Our mechanism for constructing operations by defining cases allows us to construct many operations. It is useful to be able to refer to groups of operations by name (i.e. assign names to definitions). In the above definition of *nor*, the name *nor* was assigned to three expressions that define what the name *nor* means when associated with various parameters. If we then allow an operation to be built up out of any named operations, including itself, we are in a position to define any operation that we might require. In Part II of this book we shall build up a high-level language from these primitive operations. It is important to realise that the method of definition by cases is a tool to build programs; in any computation only one case will be executed.

Since all the primitive operations are functional, and we can only define operations by means of composition of operations, and other functions, as outlined above we can say that:

Any operation is such that its output(s) are
a function of its input(s).

In the graphical notation presented earlier, functions are represented by nodes.

The functional model presented does not depend upon the arrival of data values to drive the execution. It is perfectly possible to envisage a system that is controlled by requests for data.

Consider the quadratic roots program again. We require the outputs a and b. Thus the two statements 'a := b + c', and 'b := b − c' must be evaluated. In order to do so we need to know the values of b and c. (Note we originally wanted the final value of b referred to on the left-hand side of the statement; we now require the penultimate value referred to on the right-hand side of the assignment.) Requests for these values can be passed back to the statements that generate them ('c := c / a' and 'b := − b / a'). Eventually requests can be passed back until the input values are requested. This view of the evaluation process is known as the **demand-driven** approach, since execution is controlled by the demands (requests) for data. The term **lazy evaluation** is also sometimes used, since only values that are actually needed are evaluated, and then only when they are needed, and not before [HMo76]. The implications of lazy evaluation are rather more complex than this simple explanation would seem to suggest [FWi79]. A request for a data value can in fact be interpreted as a request for a method of calculating that value. The value may or may not be used later. Evaluation is only carried out when absolutely necessary − hence the use of the term 'lazy'.

This functional model is built upon the idea of combining functions in certain ways. The programming language Lisp is often regarded as a classic example of this approach to computing, and in many ways the model we have presented may be seen as similar.

Implicit in our model, however, is the concept of functions being applied to data items, and to the results of functions. The pure functional approach of combining only functions is best reflected in Backus's FP [Bac78].

An FP system consists of:

(1) a set of **objects**. These are the basic values manipulated by the system;
(2) a set of **functions** to map objects to objects. Examples of typical functions are selector functions (to select an element of a sequence), list reversal, and the usual arithmetic functions;
(3) a single operation – **application**;
(4) a set of **functional forms** which are used to combine existing functions or objects to form new functions;
(5) a set of **definitions**, which give names to functions.

The only operation in an FP system is **application**. The power of an FP system comes from its ability to combine functions to form new functions. Four possible functional forms are:

composition $(f \circ g):x = f:(g:x)$

The composition of functions f and g applied to an object x is the same as the function f applied to the result of applying g to x.

construction $[f1, ... ,fn]:x = \langle f1:x, ... ,fn:x \rangle$

The list of functions f1 to fn applied to x is the list of results obtained by applying each f to x.

condition $(p \rightarrow f;g):x = $ if (p:x) is true then f:x; if (p:x) is false then g:x; otherwise undefined.

Either f or g is applied to x depending on whether p applied to x yields true or false.

constant $\bar{x}:y = x$, where x is an object.

Using these functional forms we can express the factorial function '!' as

$$eq0 \rightarrow \bar{1}; \times \circ [id, ! \circ sub1]$$

The functions eq0 and sub1 are defined

$$eq0 = eq \circ [id, \bar{0}]$$
$$sub1 = - \circ [id, \bar{1}]$$

(id is the identity function, $\times$ multiplication, $-$ subtraction, and eq the equality operation).

The definition of eq0 may be read as

> apply the identity operation and the 0 constant function
> giving a list of two objects — the value and zero;
> test for equality.

The definition of sub1 may be read as

> apply the identity operation, and the 1 constant function
> giving a list of two objects — the value and 1;
> perform a subtraction.

The definition of factorial may thus be read as

> apply the test 'if equals 0';
> if the answer is true then apply the 1 constant function
> (return the value 1);
> otherwise (not equal to zero) multiply the pair of values
> resulting from:
> applying the identity function, and applying factorial to
> the value less 1.

The important characteristic of FP to note is that nowhere in the program (definition of factorial) is there any mention of the value being manipulated. In other words, the characteristics of the data (type etc.) have been separated totally from the description of the actions to be performed.

We have thus totally eliminated the concepts of variables and assignments that are characteristic of the control flow model of computing.

5

Models of computing: summary

We have presented in this part of the book two basic models of computing: the control flow model, and the data flow model. We have seen how the control flow model is based on the program explicitly containing instructions to control the order of execution of operations. In the data flow model this explicit ordering has been replaced by an implicit ordering given the data dependencies. The functional approach to computing briefly introduced in the last chapter again does not include any explicit ordering. In fact it does not contain any operational information at all which gives us the option of using either a data-driven or demand-driven evaluation method. The classical data flow model is based on the operational notion of a data-driven system.

It is perhaps worth making a closer comparison of the model used in this book with the classical model of data flow as exemplified by the work at MIT (see, for example, [DeJ74] and [Rum77]).

The classical model is based on a cyclic graphical notation. The graph in Fig. 5.1 illustrates how primitive nodes may be combined in order to construct programs. We also saw earlier how cyclic graphs may be used to represent loop constructs. This is illustrated in Fig. 5.2. Cyclic graphs have two potential drawbacks. Firstly it is possible to construct deadly embraces (Fig. 5.3). If we restrict the construction of cycles to suitable ones using only switches and merges etc., then this problem can be overcome. The second problem

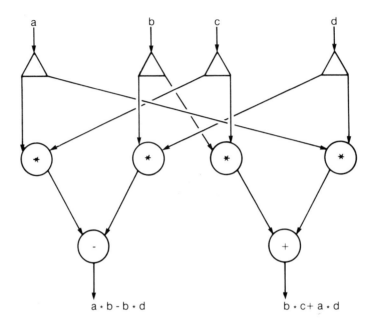

Fig. 5.1 — A simple data flow graph.

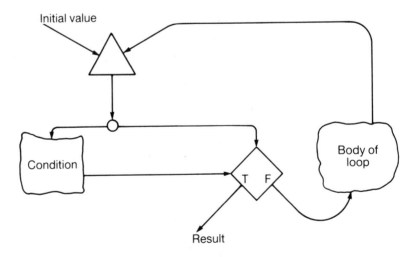

Fig. 5.2 — A cyclic data flow graph.

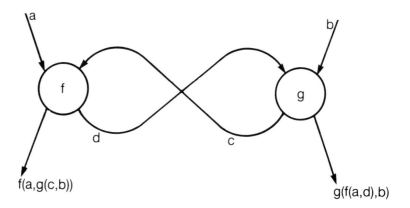

f(a,g(c,b))

g(f(a,d),b)

Fig. 5.3 — A deadly embrace in a data flow graph.

is the one of 'race' conditions. To illustrate the problem consider the
graph in Fig. 5.4 which uses Rumbaugh's notation [Rum77]. Suppose
this graph was in the body of a loop, then the two values X1 and X2
could follow each other down the input arc. The result of the conditional on X1 is to meet with Y1 at computation C, and the result
of X2 with Y2. Now assume that X1 is routed through computation
A, which takes a long time, and X2 through computation B which is
short. It is easy to see that the result of X2 may overtake the result
of X1, and thus there is a matching problem at C. X1 and X2 may be
considered to be 'racing' through parallel computations. An incorrect
result will be produced if X2 'wins' as it will be paired with Y1 and
not Y2 at computation C. This problem may be overcome by attach-
ing labels, or colours, to tokens and by ensuring that only tokens
with the same colour can be combined in any computation. In the
above example X1 and Y1 would be given one colour or label, and
X2 and Y2 a different colour or label. In computation C a check
would have to be made that its inputs both carried the same label.

Neither of these problems exist with an acyclic graphical notation.
The functional model adopted in this book uses a graphical representation only as a means of illustrating various points. The functional
model leads naturally to an acyclic graphical notation, and thus
differs from the classical graphical model in which cyclic graphs
appear to be a natural construct.

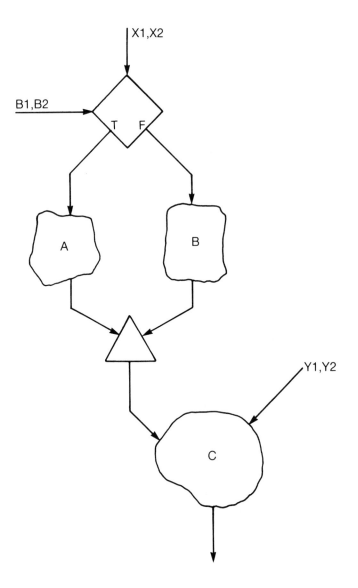

Fig. 5.4 — A 'race' condition in a data flow graph.

Part

II

LANGUAGES FOR
DATA FLOW

6

Introduction

Having developed a model of computing which allows for a large amount of concurrency, it is necessary to specify a suitable language for the design of programs. There are many different approaches to the specification of programming languages for parallel processing. The principles behind several of them are discussed in this part of the book.

We should, however, first see what features we require in our language. Ideally the language would be functional, to mirror our model, and since we are aiming at a non-sequential approach to programming we would not expect the order of function definitions to be related to their order of execution.

We should like to use structured program design techniques, so in this chapter we shall first briefly review some of the currently accepted structured program design techniques.

The much-discussed 'software crisis' has led many distinguished computer scientists to consider what techniques may be applied to the program design process in order to ensure that reliable programs, that actually do what is required of them, can be consistently produced with a minimum of effort. Much of the discussion can be traced back to Dijkstra's now famous letter to the ACM [Dij68].

A term that is frequently used when program design methodology is discussed is 'structured programming'. For the academic world the book by Dahl, Dijkstra, and Hoare [DDH72] provides a 'definition' of the approach, though to talk of a formal definition of structured programming is to a certain extent missing the point [DeP74]. More recently Michael Jackson [Jac75], and subsequently Ed Yourdon

[You75], have provided commercially oriented views of programming methodology which come under the generic title of structured programming.

Structured programming is often associated with the elimination of certain 'harmful' features such as **goto** statements [Dij68], and global variables [WSh73]. Such a definition of structured programming has now been discredited to a large extent (see, for example, [Knu74]). The harmful effects of such features may be attributable to the possible side effects which they cause or allow. The elimination of all such features could lead to the elimination of what one might consider to be the fundamental concept in traditional, von Neumann, computing, namely the variable (see [Bau76]). As we saw when we discussed the functional approach earlier it is perfectly possible to develop a model which does not contain the concept of a variable.

A basic assumption of structured programming (and other modern program design methodologies) is that the human programmer is incapable of considering a complex problem without splitting it up into more manageable sub-problems. The aim of structured programming is to develop a program in a simple and clear way from an obviously correct, but abstract version, thus ensuring that the final program is obviously correct.

The specification of a correct, well-structured, initial version is obviously a key factor in the development of a program. In data processing problems the structure of the data being processed is a fundamental consideration upon which the initial design is based. This is the basis of the approaches taken in [Jac75] and [You75].

Having defined an initial (abstract) version of the program it is necessary to refine that abstract version and produce a working program, i.e. a program at a level understandable by a computer. (In principle it is possible to refine or develop a program in either a top-down manner, as intimated above, or in a bottom-up manner, i.e. by defining various 'useful' constructs at a machine level, and then using these to build up to the abstract, high-level, initial version). A method of top-down refinement much advocated by proposers of structured programming techniques is that of stepwise refinement described in [Wir71].

The program is initially written at a high level of abstraction and then the various abstract statements are refined until the target language (be it Pascal, Algol 68, Fortran, or machine code) is reached. An important feature of stepwise refinement is that the various data structures used in a program should also be refined from a very high level of abstraction down to a suitable machine or language level.

Ideally there should be no need for the programmer to consider the nature of the language and machine (i.e. the language implementation) he is aiming at. Obviously, though, in the real world, machine and language features will influence the efficiency of the program, and thus must be borne in mind.

Stepwise refinement is to a large extent concerned with splitting the task of designing a large program into manageable sub-tasks. An alternative way of splitting a program into more manageable sections is the modular programming approach (see, for example, [Par72]).

This technique is usually associated with large projects where each module is then developed by a separate team of programmers, or by an individual. Clearly one way of splitting a program into modules to be developed by individuals would be to assign each abstract statement in an initial version to a separate person for refinement. This is unlikely to be a very successful approach, since two important criteria for the specification of modules are that their interfaces be well-defined, and also that there be no duplication of purpose between the modules (for example, we would not want two modules both concerned with disk accesses).

One of the main advantages claimed for modular design techniques is the ability to modify the original program. Assuming that the modules have been well chosen, should the program require modification at a later time, it should be possible to restrict the modifications to a limited number of modules (maybe only one) so that it is unnecessary to rewrite the whole program.

The same advantage can be claimed for stepwise refinement in that only certain refinements should need to be altered. However, a large program developed by stepwise refinement will in general be a complete program unit, and will often be compiled as one program, whereas a program developed as a set of modules is probably more easily compiled in stages. Nevertheless both methods are useful in their own right, and can indeed be successfully combined. In particular it is often the case that in a large programming project the problem may be split initially into fairly large modules, each of which is then developed using stepwise refinement.

Since a program developed by any of the 'structured' methods outlined above consists of a number of virtually autonomous parts it is possible to test parts of a program without having written the rest. It is thus easier to develop reliable and correct programs, since faults are more localised. In an unstructured program one 'operation' may be described in various parts of the program which are not textually related. (For example, when **goto** statements are used in an unstructured way, control can be transferred in a random way throughout a program.) Thus an error in the description of this particular 'operation' could be anywhere in the program, and thus be harder to locate.

It should be noted that pure top-down, or bottom-up, development is usually impossible. Inevitably some decisions that are taken will prove, at a later stage, to be wrong or undesirable. A well-structured program design should, however, enable any 'backtracking' that is necessary to be done easily, in the same way as is done when a correct program needs to be modified.

Before leaving the topic of traditional programming techniques it is perhaps worth mentioning the use of decision tables (see, for example, [Kin67]). The fundamental principle of the decision table approach is the enumeration of all possible cases along with the action required in each case. This approach can be considered to be equivalent to the method of function definition by cases that was introduced earlier.

No discussion of program design techniques would be complete without mentioning the subject of program proving. Various different approaches have been suggested (see, for example, the papers [HKi76], [RLe77], and [Gri77]). The generally accepted approach to program proving seems to be based on the idea of the state of a computation. Assertions are made about the state at various points in the program, and 'proving' the program correct entails showing that the steps of the program do actually ensure that the inserted assertions hold. Thus, as well as developing a sequential algorithm to solve the problem, the programmer has to provide a definitional solution, if he wishes to prove his program 'correct'.

In conclusion then, we have seen that all current program design methods are based upon the notion of splitting up a problem into sub-problems that are more manageable, and then solving these separately. Traditionally the splitting of the problem into sub-problems has been based on the principle that the original problem comprises a set of sequential steps. It is equally possible, however, to separate a problem into sub-problems using data dependency as the criterion. This approach is clearly more appropriate for use with the data flow model of computing.

If we wish to use the techniques outlined above, then we would expect our language to be structured in some way (cf. the traditional block structure of Algol-like languages). The methods of program design we have advocated imply that a function must be definable in terms of other functions, including itself. Indeed our model of computing also uses this idea of function composition in order to express all possible operations. Recursion is, therefore, a natural construct we would expect to see. On the other hand, loops and other cyclic constructs, being based on the notions of sequentiality and control, are less likely to appear in our notation. They are of course not essential, since it is possible to express all iterative constructs recursively.

The constraint which we introduced to prevent deadly embraces suggests, in graphical terms, that the program must be acyclic. It is this, along with the functional nature of our model, which implies that streams are not a natural concept. Combining the notion of acyclic programs with the desire for non-sequentiality suggests that some form of single assignment rule is required (see [Cha71]); that is, we assign names to values rather than values to names. It was intimated earlier that data flow led to the elimination of the variable. You will now see that the single-assignment rule leads to the elimination of the programming variable. The concept of name (or variable) which we are left with bears a much closer resemblance to the concept of a mathematical variable in that it represents a single unknown value (determined at run-time) rather than a set of values. A mathematical variable once associated with a value retains that same value throughout the computation (or proof), whereas a variable in a programming language can normally take many values, changing its value as the computation proceeds.

In summary, we would expect any high-level data flow programming language to have the following features.

(1) Any program is non-sequential (i.e. it is an unordered list of statements/definitions).
(2) The language is functional.
(3) Programs in the language obey the semantic single assignment rule.
(4) There is a name localisation (structuring) mechanism.

Furthermore we can note some features that we would expect to be absent from the design.

(1) No control constructs (for example, **goto** statements and traditional loops).
(2) No programming variables which depend upon the state of a computation. The concept of name (variable) we would expect to find is much closer to the idea of a mathematical variable.

The data flow model we have presented is, we believe, more suited to parallel processing than the traditional approach. In this part of the book we are going to present a case for the design of a new functional or applicative programming language consistent with the data flow model. Even without reference to data flow a coherent argument may be presented for a change in current programming language design; see, for example, Backus's Turing Award lecture [Bac78], where he argues for a change to a functional style of programming such as the one we propose.

7

Control flow languages

Existing programming languages are virtually all based on the control flow model of computing. In this chapter we will examine the various ways in which we could adapt these languages for use with the data flow model.

One possible approach to the task of making a language compatible with the data flow model of computing would be to develop a 'compiler' which would analyse a program written in a traditional language such as Fortran or Pascal, in an attempt to discover all the possible parallelism.

If the aim is to design a language suitable for parallel processing then this approach is unsatisfactory because it avoids the problem. There are some other approaches that try to avoid designing a totally new language which would add to the ever-increasing number of languages which the programmer has to choose from.

One approach would be to graft additional features on to an existing language in order to allow for parallelism. An example of this approach is Anderson's **fork** and **join** constructs [And65] which we looked at earlier, and decided was not acceptable. An alternative would be to design a new language which included specific parallel control features (for example, Modula [Wir77]). Many of the problems associated with the adding of new features to existing languages remain, and we would still not have a language totally consistent with the data flow approach.

Yet another approach would be to take the syntax of an existing control flow language, such as Pascal, and provide some new semantics which make it consistent with the new model of computing. A language based on the notion of control flow does not provide a particularly suitable basis for this, as we shall see:

Assignment statements
To fit in with the data flow model of computing, a single assignment rule would have to be introduced and already we have an inconsistency with the original semantics. Thus the programmer is likely to be confused by the two conflicting semantics, and the whole point of using an existing language is lost.

Functions
Functions would appear at first sight to map neatly on to a data flow model. However, such concepts as global variables (and hence 'call by reference') would have to disappear. Also procedures that rely on side-effects for their usefulness (i.e. those that do not return results, like most input/output procedures) would have to be eliminated.

Conditionals
Conditional expressions map neatly on to a data flow model, but conditional statements are less easy to re-interpret, since they are control constructs, and do not return a result but rely on assignment side-effects for their usefulness.

Iterative constructs
Some for-loops could be translated in a similar way to APL-like operators [Ive62], but basically the concept for a control statement is foreign to our model of computing. We would have to use iterative expressions, and although the semantics of a form of iterative expression has been defined in [Gla78] it is not strictly a re-interpretation of an existing language feature, but rather an additional construct; such additions were discussed earlier.

It may reasonably be argued that Pascal is not a suitable starting point for the re-interpretation of a language, and that a functional language such as Lisp would be more appropriate, though in this chapter we are really discussing purely control flow languages. Unfortunately Lisp does not naturally have the structure required by the program design methods we would like to apply. Furthermore the notation of Lisp does not readily suggest any extensions that may be made in order to introduce appropriate structuring features.

Pure Lisp [McC60] (or indeed lambda-calculus), simply as a functional notation, would provide a suitable basis for the development of a language, though we feel that the 'syntactic sugaring', with its numerous nested brackets, is not all it might be. The extended Lisp notation used as a programming language, including such strictly sequential features as the PROG function, is less appropriate for use with the data flow approach.

It is not really surprising that no control flow language is totally consistent with the data flow model. What we have seen though is that it is not at all easy to re-interpret a control flow language using data flow semantics. It seems reasonable, therefore, to consider how a totally new language, based on data flow principles, might be developed. Three options will be considered in the next few chapters. Firstly we shall consider the design of a graphical language based on the graphical notations that have been used to represent data flow programs. Secondly we shall consider the design of textual languages for use with the data flow model. Finally we shall turn again to functional languages, and consider the relationship between them and the data flow approach.

8

Graphical data flow languages

The usual data flow model of computing is based on a graphical notation for programs with nodes representing operations, and arcs representing data dependencies. It is clearly possible to use this notation as a graphical programming language.

In general a program may be represented by a directed graph. The nodes are used to represent the operations, and the arcs represent the flow of data, and show the data dependencies. Various research groups have defined their own elaborations upon this basic notation, and some of them will be discussed later. A typical representation of a program to calculate the difference of the sum and product of two numbers is given in Fig. 8.1.

Besides being used to represent an abstract program, graphs can be used to represent computations. The notion of tokens flowing down arcs is used to do this. A token is considered to carry a data value. When a node has a sufficient set of data tokens upon its input arc(s) it generates an appropriate set of data tokens upon its output arc(s). This is referred to as 'firing'. In the simplest case a sufficient set of input tokens is regarded as a complete set, and often there are restrictions about the number of tokens on an arc. For our initial notation we will allow only one token per arc, and assume that a node 'fires' when all its inputs are present. Some alternative semantic rules will be considered later. Taking the above program the use of

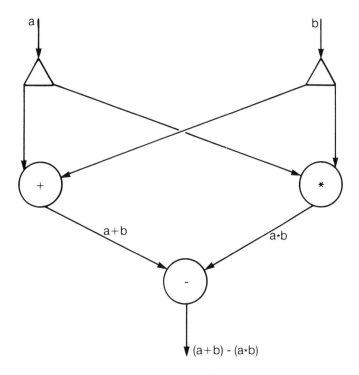

Fig. 8.1 — Program to calculate the difference between the sum and product of two numbers.

tokens can be illustrated in a series of snapshots (Fig. 8.2) which show the steps of a typical computation.

The primitive operation: *nor*
The operation *nor* may be represented by a simple node as in Fig. 8.3(a). When used in the representation of a program the node would simply be drawn as in Fig. 8.3(b) and it is understood to refer to the appropriate case in any computation.

A constant generator
A constant generator is illustrated in Fig. 8.4. The sufficient input set is empty. Therefore the node may be considered to be enabled at the start of execution, and may 'fire' as soon as the execution of the program is initiated.

A copy function
A copy function is shown in Fig. 8.5.

A general operation may be represented as in Fig. 8.6.

Earlier we introduced the concept of a deadly embrace, where two operations are dependent on the outputs of each other. It is impossible to perform either operation assuming that all inputs must be present before evaluation can take place. In order to prevent such constructions, where it is impossible to define a partial ordering on the operations, the following rule about combining operations may be introduced.

> No operations may be combined in such a manner as to cause an operation to be dependent, either directly or indirectly, upon its own output(s).

In graphical terms the graph must be acyclic.

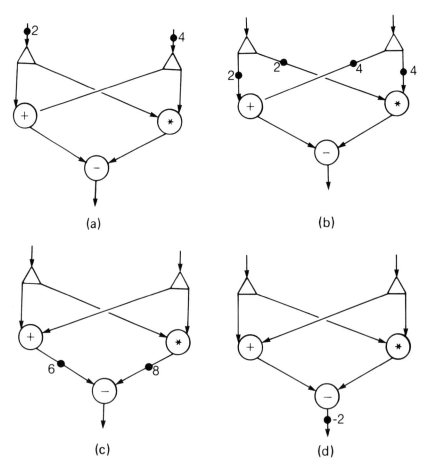

(a)

(b)

(c)

(d)

Fig. 8.2 – Snapshots illustrating stops in evaluation of a program graph. (a) Initial input tokens present. (b) Copy nodes fire. (c) Sum and product are calculated. (d) Difference is calculated.

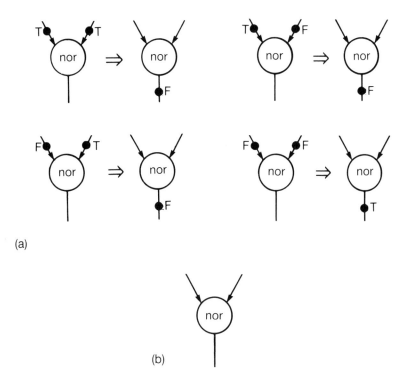

(a)

(b)

Fig. 8.3 — The *nor* node. (a) The four possible cases of inputs with appropriate outputs. (b) Representation in a program graph.

Fig. 8.4 — A constant generator.

Fig. 8.5 — A copy function.

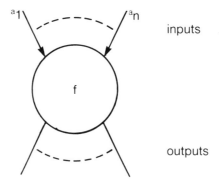

Fig. 8.6 — A general operation, f.

The problem of deadly embraces (deadlocks) is also avoidable by relaxing the condition that all inputs to an operation must be present for evaluation of that operation. Consider, first of all, operations with two inputs. The argument presented is easily extended to operations with more than two inputs.

If only one input is ever required, the deadlocked node may be expanded, and the deadlock removed. If, however, sometimes one and sometimes both inputs are required, then only at run-time can the deadlock be detected. This may be illustrated by the two rather artificial examples in Fig. 8.7. In the first example only one input is required for each compound node, and so no deadlock occurs. In the second example both compound nodes contain the multiplication operation. If one of the arguments to multiplication is zero then the result must be zero, and computation can proceed without waiting for the second argument. In this example, only if the input is non-zero will deadlock occur.

In the model presented in this book, little (if anything) would be gained by allowing cyclic graphs with deadlock detection at run-time. All that might be gained is the possibility of allowing a series of values to flow down an arc (in graphical terms). With the full generality of function definition which is allowed, such a facility is not necessary since a series of values may be represented by a function definition. This argument does not mean that nothing can be gained by relaxing the condition that a sufficient input set is a complete set, and this possibility will be discussed further in a later chapter.

The graphical notation introduced so far is incomplete, in the sense that there is no way of representing the concept of definition by cases. One way to do this is to introduce the union node and case

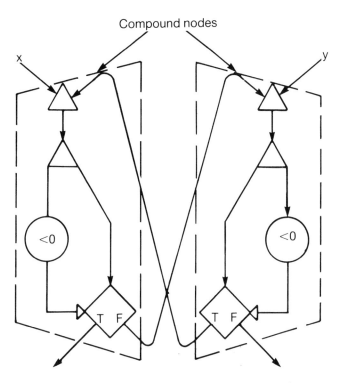

Fig. 8.7(a) — Program graph where apparent deadlock can be avoided by relaxing input conditions (only one input is needed for each sub-graph).

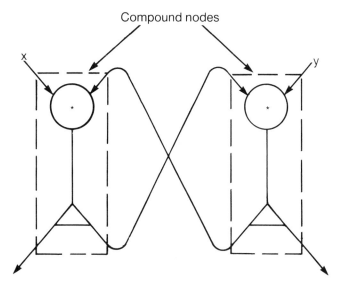

Fig. 8.7(b) — Program graph where deadlock may or may not occur, depending upon input values.

nodes as in Fig. 8.8. (Note the method of defining a sub-graph.) This represents:

$$abs = [a : \{x \mid x < 0\}] \; negate(a),$$
$$abs = [a : \{x \mid x >= 0\}] \; a$$

The idea is that a data value is passed through a case node only if the condition (predicate) given in the node is true. A union node accepts only one of its inputs and produces it as output. If only one input arrives then that is the one selected. If both inputs arrive then the union node behaves in a non-deterministic fashion, and selects one or other of the inputs randomly. The representation of an arc by a dotted line indicates that at run-time data may or may not 'flow' down this path; the notation is usually reserved for arcs immediately adjacent to union and case nodes (or their equivalent), otherwise large parts of a program graph would have a tendency to consist solely of dotted lines, and their purpose would have been lost.

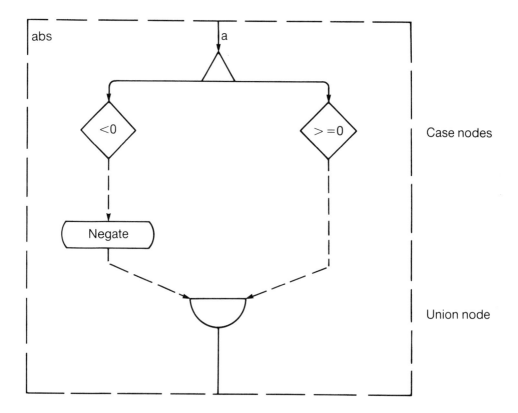

Fig. 8.8 — Definition by cases using union and case nodes.

An alternative graphical notation may be regarded as modelling more closely the likely evaluation mechanism for functions defined by cases, by illustrating the likely order of evaluation of individual operations. In this notation, 'pass gates' are defined, which may or may not let through one of their inputs (their data input) depending upon the value of their other input (their control input). Two forms of pass gate are possible; true gates and false gates. The above *abs* function is represented using this notation in Fig. 8.9. Functional definitions of these new nodes are given below, where U is the universal set.

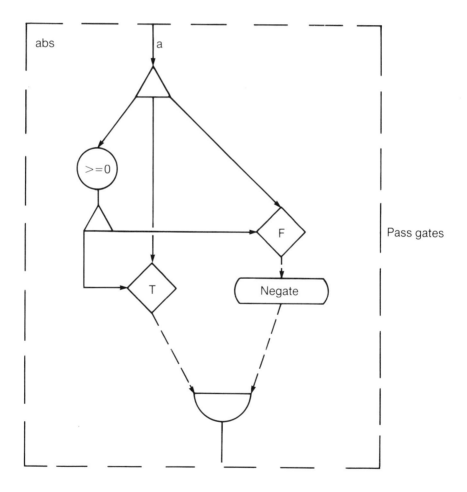

Fig. 8.9 — Definition by cases using pass gates.

union = [a : U\NULL, b : NULL] a,
union = [a : NULL, b : NULL] NULL,
union = [a : NULL, b : U\NULL] b,
union = [a : U\NULL, b : U\NULL] 'a or b'

truegate = [a : TRUE , b : U] b,
truegate = [b : FALSE, b : U] NULL

The definition of a falsegate is obvious.

A third alternative graphical notation generalises the notion of pass-gates above to 'key gates', which have a third input (usually a constant) which defines what value the control input must have to enable the data to be passed through. Figure 8.10 shows how this notation could be used to represent our example.

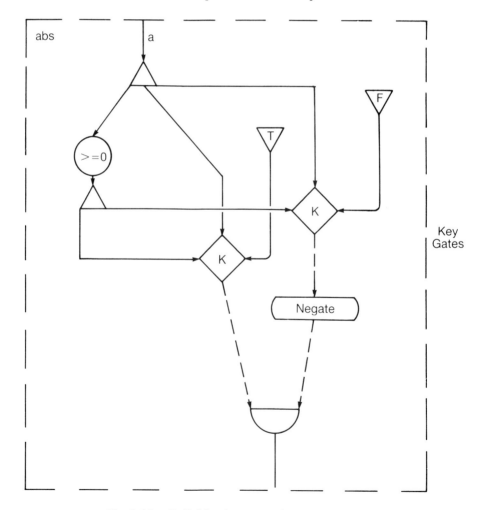

Fig. 8.10 — Definition by cases using key gates.

All these notations assume a data driven (push) model with data flowing from the top of the graph to the bottom driving the execution. There is an alternative model called the demand-driven (pull) model, in which requests for data are propagated up the graph from the bottom to the top. With the above graphical representations, a pull would cause the negate node to be invoked even if it were not necessary for it to be executed. It may, therefore, be better to place the pass gates (for example) just before the union, as shown in Fig. 8.11. For a pull model, the pull will be propagated only if the control is of the right value.

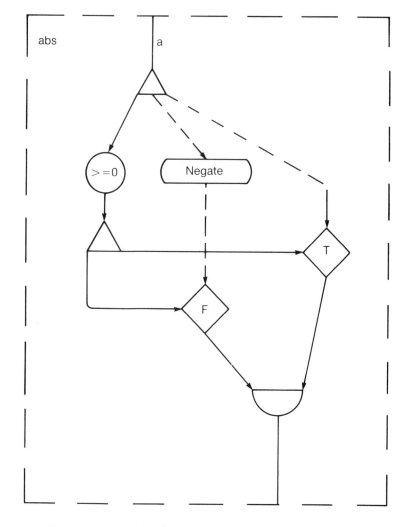

Fig. 8.11 — Definition by cases for pull model (using pass gates).

Finally, it should be noted that each evaluation (activation) of a function is regarded as a separate invocation of a function. (i.e., a conceptually distinct copy of the graph is used.)

It has been implied that, to represent a function graphically, all that is required is for the name of the function to be written inside a node. This is not an adequate method in all cases. For example, consider the following definition of a function, apply, which takes three parameters and applies the first to the last two. The first parameter, op, is a function requiring two arguments. The last two parameters, a and b, are used as the arguments to op.

apply = [op:REAL × REAL → REAL, a: REAL, b: REAL] op(a,b)

op is a formal parameter which is also a function name. There seems to be no way of representing the above definition adequately using the current graphical notation; the parameter name cannot just be written inside a node, since this does not conform to the present parameter mechanism (see Fig. 8.12).

To enable the function of Fig. 8.12 to be represented realistically it is necessary to introduce the notion of a function application node as in Fig. 8.13 (cf. [Rum77]). Now, to be consistent, all function applications ought to be made explicit. Therefore, the representation of an add node should be as shown in Fig. 8.14.

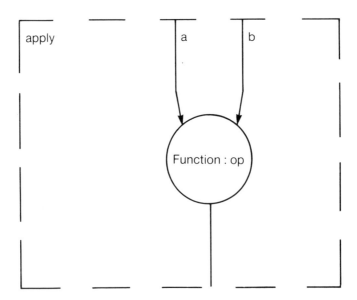

Fig. 8.12 — An attempt at representing an apply node.

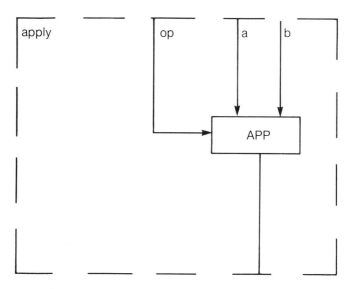

Fig. 8.13 — An explicit function application node.

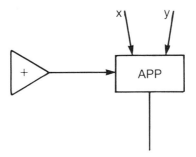

Fig. 8.14 — Representing the add operation using an explicit apply node.

Is this method of representing functions graphically adequate? The answer depends upon the semantics of the apply node. Two possible meanings will be considered initially. These are graph substitution and partial evaluation.

Firstly, suppose that an apply node was replaced by the graph of the function whenever the parameters required were presented. Thus if the above apply function were called as below:

result = apply(x, 3, 2)

where x has been defined:

x = [a: REAL, b:REAL] (a + b) * (a − b)

then the original graph would be as in Fig. 8.15(a). Figure 8.15(b) shows the expanded graph and the meaning is obvious.

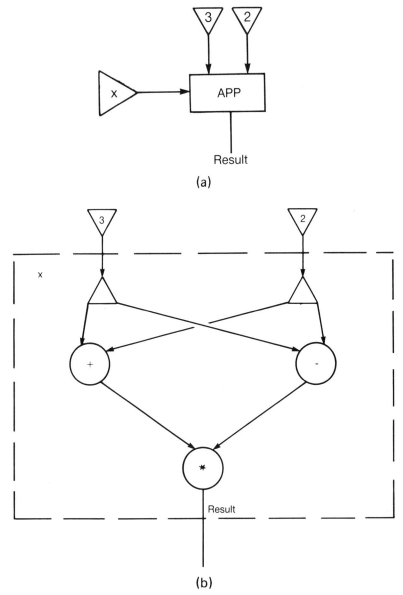

(a)

(b)

Fig. 8.15 — A simple example of function application. (a) Before graph expansion. (b) After graph expansion.

Now consider what would have happened if x had been defined as below:

x = [a: REAL, b:REAL] (a + b, a − b)

the graph could be expanded as in Fig. 8.16, but clearly something strange is happening at the output interface.

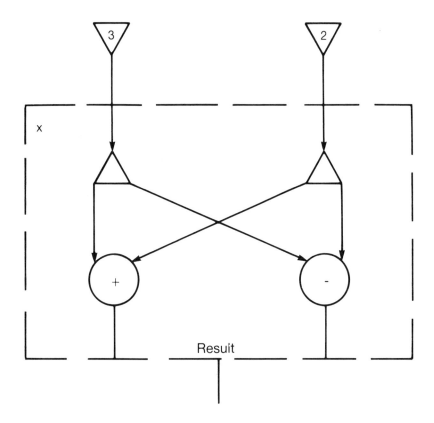

Fig. 8.16 — A more complex example of function application.

What is happening becomes clearer when it is realised that:

$(a + b, a - b)$

is really shorthand for two function definition cases:

[index: 1] a + b,
[indcx: 2] a − b

The output from the apply node is a function rather than a simple value. In the model presented in this book, this will often be the case. Even simple integers can be regarded as functions. The simple macro-expansion semantics for the apply node are clearly inadequate.

The problem is solved if a second possible semantic definition of the apply node (partial evaluation) is adopted. What is meant by this is that the result of the evaluation of an apply node is the function definition produced by evaluating the given function as far as possible by using the given parameters.

It is now possible to introduce a third possible semantic definition for the apply node. Suppose it is defined merely to be a process of binding the given parameters to the given function. Thus the output is a function definition with some actual parameters tied to it. Conceptually, evaluation only needs to take place when the value of the final output function is to be presented to the human user. Evaluation is therefore required only at the interface with the real world. From an implementor's viewpoint partial evaluation may be more attractive, but conceptually the delayed evaluation model seems neater. Therefore, we shall no longer refer to apply nodes, but rather to 'associate nodes', which merely associate (or bind) actual parameters to function definitions. An implicit evaluation node will be assumed at the output interface of all programs. If each case of a function definition is expanded with associated parameters, then recursive definitions would clearly lead to infinite expansions. As a formal model this is perfectly acceptable, but as an implementation technique it is unacceptable.

Alternative data flow models
As we mentioned earlier data flow research has been under way since about 1970. Four early notations are presented in [Ada70], [DeJ74], [Rum77], and [Kos73]. Most subsequent work has been based on Dennis's notation [DeJ74]. It is, however, worthwhile mentioning some of the features included in the other models. The notations they developed may be considered to represent alternative graphical programming languages. In Chapter 3 we briefly introduced Rumbaugh's notation for representing data flow programs graphically [Rum77]. We will now look at some of the variations suggested by other workers.

Synchronisation
Both MIT notations ([DeJ74], [Rum77]) insist on synchronising the execution of operations by having all inputs present before execution. On the other hand Adams [Ada70] allows for, and Kosinski [Kos73] defines, operations that may execute with partial inputs, and indeed may take more than one input from the same arc.

Adams allows multiple tokens to reside on arcs, and suggests a queueing mechanism to ensure the correct order of evaluation. Although the MIT workers only allow one token on an arc at once, the possibility of cyclic graphs means that a colouring, or labelling, mechanism is required to ensure that tokens are correctly matched for evaluation. Adams and Kosinski have different methods of control; Adams uses the graph terminology of edges for arcs, and uses the concept of locked and unlocked edges for control. In Kosinski's notation, however, the arcs not only carry data values, but also control signals PRESENCE and DONE in order to synchronise the operations.

Run-time data-dependent decision mechanisms

We have already shown how Rumbaugh introduces the concept of run-time data-dependent decisions in Chapter 3. Rumbaugh used Dennis's work as a starting point and tried to simplify the set of nodes required. He assumed that, to produce well-formed data flow graphs, switches and merge nodes must always be used in a controlled manner. This assumption seems to be justified. Dennis, on the other hand, uses some rather more general nodes, as illustrated in Fig. 8.17.

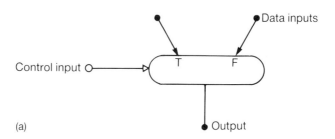

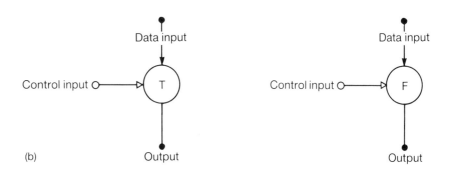

Fig. 8.17 — Nodes for run-time data-dependent decisions in Dennis's notation. (a) The merge node. Which input arc the output token is taken from depends upon the value (true or false) of the token on the control input. (b) T- and F-gates. An output token (of value equal to the input token) is placed on the output arc if the value of the control token is true (for a T-gate) or false (for an F-gate).

We show in Fig. 8.18 how conditional and while-loop constructs may be programmed using Dennis's nodes. (Note that it is now necessary to have an initial token on an arc in the loop graph.)

It should be noted that Rumbaugh's nodes are more suited to expressing the constructs shown in Figs. 8.18(a) and 8.18(b), but are not as general, or powerful (in some cases), as Dennis's.

Adams [Ada70] also uses two sorts of nodes:

(1) Select and route (roughly equivalent to Dennis's merge node).
(2) Conditional (and negative conditional) route (roughly equivalent to Dennis's T- and F-gates).

Kosinski [Kos73] has a more interesting choice of control nodes. He generalises Dennis's merge gate to an inbound switch which allows the programmer to use values other than just booleans as control inputs (in the same way that the case statement is a generalisation of

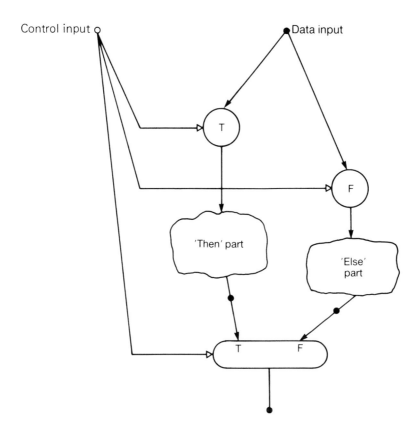

Fig. 8.18(a) — A conditional construct.

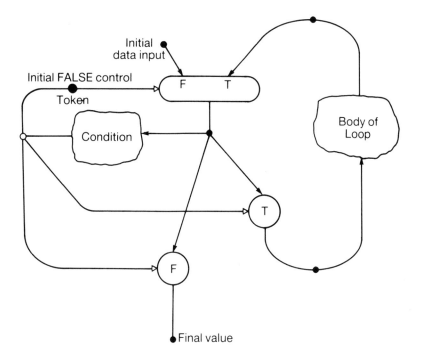

Fig. 8.18(b) — A while loop.

the conditional statement). He also defines an outbound switch which is a generalisation of Rumbaugh's switch in the same sort of way.

These are mere generalisations of the MIT approaches and not particularly interesting in themselves.

Clearly conditional and loop constructs could be built up just using these nodes as before. Kosinski, however, introduces a special loop control node (see Fig. 8.19).

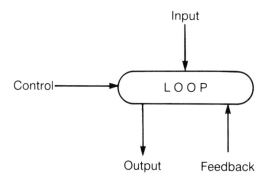

Fig. 8.19 — Kosinski's loop control node.

The loop starts when a datum arrives on the input path. This datum is then placed on the output path along with a PRESENCE synchronisation signal. When an input is received on the control path it is retained within the operator and a DONE control signal is sent back on the control path. When a datum is received on the feedback path a choice is made. If the control value received was TRUE then the datum received by the operator on the feedback path is sent out on the output path and the cycle repeats. Otherwise if FALSE was received on the control path the loop terminates by sending DONE on the initial path.

A while loop constructed from the loop node is shown in Fig. 8.20.

The loop node can also be used to construct memory nodes, which is not done in any other notation (see later).

Functions

Two basic approaches to the representation of functions are possible. The first alternative is that any sub-graph may be named and used as a function. This is the approach adopted by Kosinski [Kos73], and

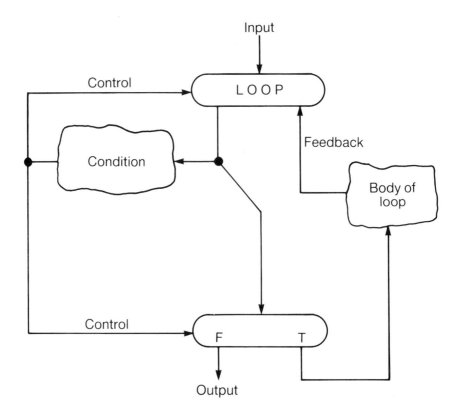

Fig. 8.20 – A while loop using Kosinski's loop control node.

implicitly by Adams [Ada70]. At MIT ([DeJ74], [Rum77]) the alternative approach of using explicit function application nodes has been adopted. An alternative that we discussed earlier is to use the notion of an 'apply' node in order to allow for the passing of functions as parameters. As we explained earlier the notion of application may be replaced by one of association. The idea that any sub-graph may be defined as a function is still retained.

Memory

As mentioned before Kosinski's loop node allows him to introduce a memory node. The graph in Fig. 8.21 illustrates how a memory node may be constructed.

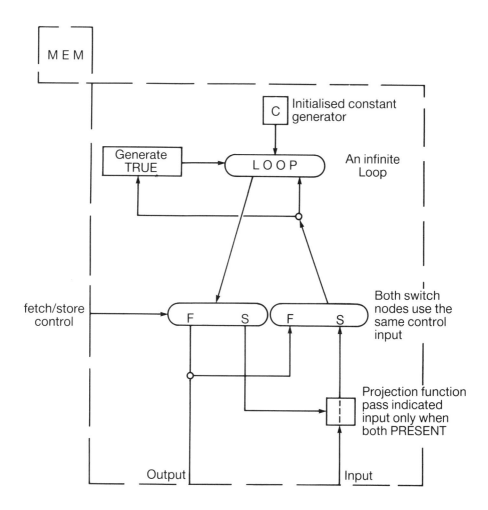

Fig. 8.21 – A memory graph.

Dennis has defined a complex structure memory involving the manipulation of pointers which is consistent with his method of applying functions explicitly.

In the functional data flow model presented in this book no explicit memory management system has been presented. This is because we have chosen to regard every object in the model to be represented by functions. Thus data to be 'remembered' is simply represented by function definitions.

9

Textual data flow
languages

So far in this book we have presented a model of computing, the data flow model, which allows for a large degree of concurrency. In Chapter 7 it was argued that the adaptation of control flow languages was not a satisfactory solution to our desire for an appropriate programming notation. In the last chapter a graphical programming notation was presented. Clearly, at the moment, most programming languages are textual, and it therefore seems appropriate to consider what sort of textual notation may be developed for use as a data flow programming language. An interesting alternative avenue of research would be the development of graphical program design tools, along the lines of current computer-aided design systems. Such a possibility is unfortunately outside the scope of this book.

In this chapter we shall illustrate how the functional model outlined earlier may be built up to a suitable programming language level. Some suggestions for shorthand, or alternative, notations will be made in passing. The language is presented in more detail in the author's thesis [Sha82]. It is a development of a notation designed at Westfield College by Chris Hankin and the author. Originally known as HASAL [HSh77] it was implemented as part of an SERC-supported research project and became known as Cajole [HOS78]. The latest version of the Westfield College Group's language Cajole is described by Hankin and Glaser in [HGl81].

We shall also consider some of the other data flow programming languages that have been developed by various research groups.

The semantics of other non-procedural languages such as Lucid [AWa77] could also be defined using our model, but it would be a less easy task since they are not directly based on the data flow concepts presented in this book, and all of them tend to have additional features that do not have an obvious meaning in data flow. This is the topic of Chapter 10.

There is a sense in which any language could be used with the data flow model of computing since it is possible to express all functions in all languages. However, it is not the case that there needs to be a strong equivalence between a data flow program and a program to compute the same function written in any other language.

Since the functions in our model have no side-effects, it should be possible to define a non-procedural (non-sequential) notation such that the order of definitions does not signify any order of execution. This was one of our stated aims for a language for parallel processing, and seems compatible with our notion of data flow, as opposed to control flow.

Domains and data types

Our basic domain is $B \cup \{NULL\}$. That is the union of the boolean domain $\{TRUE, FALSE\}$ and the NULL value. The types integer (INT), real (REAL), and character (CHAR) can be introduced as fundamental though, in principle, they, and any other data type, can be built up in the following manner from the basic domain already used.

Recalling our note on the equivalence of the sets B and Bi, let us merely use an arbitrary set of two distinguishable elements, and refer to it as B with elements 0 and 1.

We can define the integer value 0 as

$$0 = [\ ] \ 0$$

and then define the positive integers, for example, as successors of 0.

A successor function may be defined as below:

$$\text{succ} = [a : B^n \times 0] \ (a(1:n)::1),$$
$$\text{succ} = [a : B^n \times 1] \ (\text{succ}(a(1:n))::0),$$
$$\text{succ} = [a : 0] \ 1,$$
$$\text{succ} = [a : 1] \ (1, 0),$$
$$1 = \text{succ} \ (0)$$

Note. The notation of B^n is defined later (p. 134). The notions of slicing (1:n), and catenation (::) are defined on p. 83.

Such an approach, although theoretically neat and concise, would probably not be the practical approach taken in a machine implementation. The usual method of regarding integers etc. as primitive would presumably be adopted. It matters little to the programmer which approach is actually used, and we may assume that the types INT, REAL, and CHAR either exist as primitives or have been defined as functions.

Fundamental operations

The basic arithmetic functions may be built up from the primitive *nor* function using combinatorial logic. It is, however, more convenient to represent them as infix operators, as is done in most high-level languages. In the high-level notation the programmer will be unaware of the fact that the operations and data types that he regards as fundamental have, in fact, been defined in terms of more primitive operations and types.

Aggregate data

A vector such as (3, 5, 1, 56, 2, 7) may be regarded as a one-to-one mapping from the set {1, 2, 3, 4, 5, 6} to the set {1, 2, 3, 5, 7, 56}. (Other vectors may be many-to-one.) Thus vectors may also be regarded as functions defined by cases. More complex data structures could also be defined in a similar manner. Operations on complex data types would, however, have to be defined as functions acting upon functions (and returning functions) rather than as functions acting upon primitive data. This is, in fact, already the case with simple arithmetic operations if we regard integers as being defined as functions.

We can now see that a data flow language may be defined as purely functional, since all things (data and operations) can be defined in functional terms.

Run-time data-dependent decision mechanisms

The mechanism of definition by cases which we introduced earlier allows us to make run-time data-dependent decisions in the evaluation of functions by selecting the appropriate case of the defined function. Since the major thesis of the model being discussed is that everything is defined in functional terms, it should not be necessary to introduce any other decision mechanism.

As an example, consider the following definition of a maximum function.

$$max = [a : REAL, b : REAL]\ submax(a-b, a, b),$$
$$submax = [x : \{x \mid x > 0\}, a, b]\ a$$
$$submax = [x : \{x \mid x <= 0\}, a, b]\ b$$

In a high-level programming language a 'guarded expression' mechanism such as that used in the various versions of Cajole may prove more amenable to the programmer. The concept of a guard was introduced by Dijkstra in [Dij76]. An interesting parallel development is discussed in [USc78]. In its simplest form a guarded expression consists of two expressions. The first, the guard, is a boolean expression. If its value is TRUE then the value of the guarded expression is the value of the second expression. If the guard is FALSE the guarded expression has a NULL value.

Using the notation used in the author's version of Cajole [Sha82] the maximum function would be written:

$$max = [a : REAL, b : REAL] \{a > b : a; \ a <= b : b\}$$

In this example a list of two guarded expressions has been used. If the guard 'a > b' evaluates to true then the value of the list is taken to be the value of 'a'. If the guard 'a <= b' evaluates to true then the value of the list is taken as the value of 'b'.

Any guarded expression list can be translated to functional form as follows:

$$func = [p1,....pN] \ \{guard1 \ : exp1 \ ;$$
$$guard2 \ : exp2 \ ;$$
$$\vdots \qquad \vdots$$
$$\vdots \qquad \vdots$$
$$\vdots \qquad \vdots$$
$$guardM : expM$$
$$\}$$

is equivalent to:

func = [p1,......,pN] subfunc(guard1,...,guardM,
                                    p1,.........,pN),
subfunc = [guard1 : TRUE, guard2 : FALSE,...,guardM : FALSE,
                    p1,....,pN] exp1,
subfunc = [guard1 : FALSE, guard2 : TRUE, guard3 : FALSE,
                    ......guardM : FALSE, p1,....,pN] exp2,
$$\vdots$$
$$\vdots$$
$$\vdots$$
subfunc = [guard1 : FALSE,...,guardM−1 : FALSE, guardM : TRUE,
                    p1,....,pN] expM

So far we have assumed that each of the guards (cases) are mutually exclusive. This ensures that the function is determinate. It is possible to introduce non-determinancy by relaxing this condition so that if many guards evaluate to TRUE (i.e. many cases of a function definition apply), only one result is accepted, and which result is accepted is non-determinate.

It is equally possible to define determinate solutions to the problem of guards that are not mutually exclusive. The evaluation of the guards may be ordered (cf. McCarthy conditionals [McC60]) or a set of results may be produced.

It is worth emphasising again that guarded expressions are introduced only to aid readability, and as a notational aid to the programmer. The method of 'definition by cases' is totally adequate.

Program development and name localisation

The method of program design discussed earlier, and applied to data flow programming, naturally requires some form of qualification clause to be used (cf. the auxiliary clauses of ISWIM in [Lan66]). For example, in the first definition of the function max given above, the definition,

$$max = [a : REAL, b : REAL] \ submax(a - b, a, b)$$

is 'qualified' by the definitions of submax. They could thus be written:

$$max = [a : REAL, b : REAL] \ submax \ (a - b, a, b)$$
$$WITH \ submax = [x : \{x \mid x > 0\}, a, b] \ a,$$
$$submax = [x : \{x \mid x <= 0\}, a, b] \ b$$
$$WEND$$

where the WITH..WEND clause is a qualifying clause. The scope of the definition of submax is restricted to the definition of max. Thus we have a name localisation mechanism.

The definition of a function is usually assumed to be 'constant', or unique in a given program. Since in our model a program consists solely of a set of functions we have the concept of all values being uniquely defined. Thus we have the notion of a single-assignment rule which would seem to lead to a proliferation of names even for non-trivial problems. The concept of qualifying clauses outlined above provides a convenient, and natural, name localisation mechanism that overcomes this problem.

We have now introduced the four features which we said we would expect to find in a language suitable for parallel processing. These were:

(1) any program is non-sequential;
(2) the language is functional;

(3) programs written in the language obey the single-assignment rule;
(4) there is a name localisation mechanism.

Furthermore, we have introduced a notation in which these features are a natural development from the basic concepts.

In an early version of Cajole [HOS78] we introduced the concept of a bootstrapping mechanism which, to a limited extent, made the language extensible. The main difference between this mechanism and the standard function definition facility was the ability to place function parameters in context in the construct name. Such a mechanism would enable us to build up the use of infix operators and guarded expression lists from the basic primitive functions. In any usable system, such basic extensions would be provided as system functions, but additional user-defined extensions would enable the user to tailor the system to his own requirements in a logical and clear manner.

Functions returning names

An earlier version of our data flow language [HSh77] allowed for functions that returned names as results, and which therefore could be used on the left-hand side of definitions. This possibility is not strictly necessary and may be regarded merely as an alternative, possibly neater, way of expressing some functions.

As an example, consider the following definitions of a name-returning function. Note that we do not have any specific notation to indicate that a character string is a name rather than a reference to a value required, since this possibility is not going to be included in our final language. In the following example, a5 and a6 are assumed to be names and not references to values.

$$a = [x : 5] \; a5,$$
$$a = [x : 6] \; a6.$$

This may be 'called' as below:

$$a(6) = b,$$
$$a(5) = c.$$

Now $a(6) = b$ is equivalent to:

$$([x : 5] \; a5)(6) = b \text{ and } ([x : 6] \; a5)(6) = b$$

which is equivalent to:

$$a5 = ([x : 5] \; b)(6) \text{ and } a6 = ([x : 6] \; b)(6)$$

and similarly for $a(5) = c$.

In each case only one right-hand side expression will return a value, and thus only one value will be assigned to each of a5 and a6.

Some examples

To complete this section we shall present some example programs. The first two examples concern the familiar problem of sorting.

First of all let us consider how we might define a function which would return as its result the nth element of a given vector after the vector had been sorted. We shall use the method of bubble sorting to sort the vector into decreasing order. Smaller elements are 'bubbled' up to the end of the vector, and therefore in order to find the nth element of the sorted vector we need only to perform s − n 'bubbles', where s is the length (size) of the vector.

For a first version of the program we wish to define a function bubsort which has as parameters a vector vec, and an integer n to act as the index. Let us assume that it makes use of a function vecsort which applies the bubble sort technique to the vector s − n times. Our version 1 is therefore:

$$\text{bubsort} = [\text{vec} : \{1..u\} \rightarrow \text{INT}, n : \text{INT}] \quad \text{vecsort}(\text{vec}, n)(n)$$

This defines the function bubsort with two parameters. The second parameter is of type INTeger, and the first is defined to have a type which is a mapping; that is, given a value between l and u as a parameter it will deliver an INTeger as a result. This use of a mapping type illustrates how data structures may be used. In this case the parameter vec is the functional equivalent to an array of integers indexed by values in the l to u. The function vecsort clearly uses the same two types of parameter and delivers something that also has a type that is a mapping. That is, it delivers a function that requires (at least) one parameter of type INTeger. This is why there are two sets of parameters on the right-hand side. In conventional terminology the function vecsort takes as its parameters an array to be sorted (vec), and the index (n) of the required entry in the sorted array. It returns a partially sorted array and therefore has to be indexed by n in order to return the desired value.

We now need to refine this abstract program by defining the function vecsort. The function vecsort returns either the given vector 'bubbled' once (if n is the upper bound of the vector), or the vector bubbled s − n times (s = l − u). We follow the Pascal convention of using < > to represent not equal.

vecsort = [vec: {1..u} → INT, n:INT] {n = u : bubble(vec);

n < > u : vecsort(bubble(vec),

n+1)}

This method of defining a recursive function implements an iterative computation (i.e. a computation that involves repeatedly performing the same operation). Such computations occur very frequently in programming, and thus this method of defining recursive functions is a useful standard technique. We now need to refine the program further by defining the function bubble which requires one INTeger delivering function as a parameter.

```
bubble = [vec : {l..u}→ INT]
        {u − 1 < 2 : {vec(l) > vec(u) : vec(l:u);
                      vec(l) <= vec(u) : (vec(u) :: vec(l))
                     };
         u − 1 <= 2 : {vec(l) > vec(l+1) : (vec(l) ::
                                            bubble(vec(l+1:u)));
                       vec(l) <= vec(l+1) : (vec(l+1) ::
                                            bubble((vec(l)::vec(l+2:u))))
                      }
        }
```

Now let us present the whole program.

```
bubsort = [vec : {l..u}→ INT, n : INT] vecsort (vec, n) (n)
    WITH
    vecsort = [vec : {l..u}→ INT, n : INT]
            {n = u : bubble (vec);
             n <> u : vecsort (bubble (vec), n+1)
            }
        WITH
        bubble = [vec : {l..u}→ INT]
                {u − 1 < 2 : {vec(l) > vec(u) : vec(l:u);
                              vec(l) <= vec(u) : (vec(u) :: vec(l))
                             };
                 u − 1 >= 2 : {vec(l) > vec(l+1) :
                               (vec(l)::bubble(vec(l+1:u)));
                               vec(l) <= vec(l+1) :
                               (vec(l+1)::bubble(vec(l)::
                                               vec(l+2:u))))
                              }
                }
        WEND
    WEND
```

In the above definition of bubble we have used the operator :: for catenation. This operator may be defined as below:

$$:: = [a : \{l1..u1\} \rightarrow INT, b : \{l2..u2\} \rightarrow INT]$$
$$([index : \{l1..(u1+u2-l2+1)\} \rightarrow INT]$$
$$\{index <= u1 : a(index) \ ;$$
$$index > u1 : b(index-u1-1+l2)$$
$$\}$$

index(a : b) is equivalent to:

$$index = [x] \ \{x < a : ERROR \ ;$$
$$x > b : ERROR \ ;$$
$$x >= a \ AND \ x <= b : index(x)$$
$$\}$$

The ERROR value may either cause a run-time failure or be used by the programmer to handle error conditions.

There is not much parallelism in the above sort program apart from the possibility of overlapping calls of the function vecsort. This is because the bubble sort technique is inherently a sequential technique. An alternative sort technique might be to continually split the given vector into two, sort each of the two resultant vectors, and then perform a merge sort on the two sorted vectors. When the vectors to be sorted are either one or two elements the sorting process is trivial. This method of sorting clearly exposes a much greater degree of parallelism. A program for this sorting method is given below. The operator '/' represents integer division.)

```
parsort =  [a : {l..u} → INT]
           {l=u      : a(l) ;
           u-l > 1 : merge( parsort(a(l:(u+l)'/'2)),
                                 parsort(a((u+l)'/'2+1:u))));
           u-l = 1 : {a(l) >= a(u) : a(l:u) ;
                         a(l) <   a(u) : (a(u)::a(l))
                         }
           }
        WITH
        merge = [a : {al..au} → INT, b : {bl..bu} → INT]
                {a(al)  >  b(bl) :
                   {au  =  al : (a(al)::b(b(bl:bu)) ;
                    au <> al : (a(al)::merge(a(al+1:au),b))
                   };
```

```
a(al) <= b(bl):
  {bu  =  bl : (b(bl)::a(al:au)) ;
   bu <> bl : (b(bl)::merge(a, b(bl+1:bu)))
  }
}
```
WEND

For the next example let us consider a simple mesh problem. We wish to calculate all the values of the mesh $u_{i,j,t}$ where $i = 1..I$, and $j = 1..J$ given the equation

$$u_{i,j,t} = (u_{i+1,j,t-1} + u_{i-1,j,t-1} + u_{i,j+1,t-1} + u_{i,j-1,t-1}) / 4$$

Initial values are given for all $u_{i,j,0}$ where i varies from $0..I+1$, and j varies from $0..J+1$. t is assumed to vary from 0 to T. T is taken as an input parameter. We have thus simplified the usual problem where a test for convergence is included. This was done to make the example easier to follow.

The set of values with $i = 0$ or $I+1$, or $j = 0$ or $J+1$ are regarded as boundary values which do not change throughout the computation.

The obvious approach, to avoid the unnecessary repetition of computation implied by the simple recursive definition, is to apply a function (mesh function) to the given values ($u_{i,j,0}$) T times. In [Bir80] Bird discusses the avoidance of unnecessary repetition of computation in such recursive definitions by a method he terms tabulation. This approach can be considered to be related to the idea of adding guards which will be discussed later. By adopting tabulation (or a variation on it) the simple recursive definition would be an acceptable program.

Using the same method of defining a recursive function to perform an iterative computation that we had before, we can write:

```
answer = mesh function (given values, T)
    WITH
    mesh function = [value: {0..I+1}×{0..J+1} →  REAL,
                                                time: INT]
                      {time = 0 : value ;
                       time <> 0 : mesh function(next values,
                                                      time−1)

                      }
    WEND
```

To define nextvalues all we need to do is define a function with two integer parameters (as indexers), using the equation given.

nextvalues = [a : {0..I+1} b : {0..J+1}]
$\quad$ {a = 0 OR a = I+1 OR b = 0 OR b = J+1 :
$\qquad$ value (a, b) ;
$\quad$ a <> 0 AND a <> I+1 AND b <> 0 AND <> J+1 :
$\qquad$ (value(a−1,b) + value(a+1,b) +
$\qquad$ value(a,b−l) + value(a,b+1)) / 4
$\quad$ }

The above definition of nextvalues would, of course, be placed in a qualification clause.

The specification of the final problem is taken directly from [PRe76].

'Assume that we have a complete street map of a city. In addition, we also have the exact locations of a number of key points, which have been arbitrarily distributed throughout the city. Each key point has a unique name.

'We wish to store all the above information as a computer-access-ible database such that we can write a program that would accept as input the following two items of information:

an arbitrary address <u>a</u> within the city
a number r

and would output:

the names of all keypoints that lie in a circle of radius r centred at <u>a</u>.'

We note one further paragraph from the original problem statement.

'When drawing a circle of radius r, you may round it up to the nearest block, or you may even replace the circle with another type of template (for example, a rectangle) if this facilitates your solution.'

The input set (i.e. the given data) may be summarised as:

M — the map of the city
Ka — the list of key points in the city
<u>a</u> — an arbitrary address
r — the radius

M and Ka form a permanent database, and <u>a</u> and r are user inputs. The output required is simply the set:

Kt — a list of keypoints within distance r of <u>a</u> in M.

In our notation we can represent the first version of the program by:

Kt = select within range (M, Ka, a, r)

Following the technique used in [PRe76] we decide that M, a, and r are used to produce a template T, and then each keypoint in Ka is examined to see if it is within T. The function 'select within range' can thus be refined:

select within range = [map, points, address, radius]
       test if contained(points,
             template(map,address,radius))

It is now necessary to make some assumptions about M, Ka, and a. We shall assume that:

(1) a cartesian coordinate system is used;
(2) the map is completely within the positive quadrant;
(3) a rectangular template can be used (actually square 2r × 2r);
(4) the map is rectangular.

For the generation of the template, we need to know the bounds of the map and the coordinates of a. We shall use (x1, x2), (y1, y2), and (ax, ay) respectively.

  All we need to know about the template are its bounds. Thus we have (using a guarded expression list notation):

template = [x1, x2, y1, y2, ax, ay, r]
     ({ax–r < x1 : x1 ; ax–r >= x1 : ax–r},
      {ax+r < x2 : x2 ; ax+r >= x2 : ax+r},
      {ay–r < y1 : y1 ; ay+r >= y1 : ay–r},
      {ay+r < y2 : y2 ; ay+r >= y2 : ay+r })

We need to refine the function 'test if contained'. We assume Ka to be a function, $\{1..n\} \times \{1,2\} \to INT \times INT$. A recursive definition is then called for:

test if contained = [points : {1..u} × {1,2},
       x1 : INT, x2 : INT, y1 : INT, y2 : INT]
       {l = u : this one ;
        l <> u : (this one,
        test if contained(points(l+1:u),x1,x2,y1,y2))
       }

     WITH
     this one = {points(count,1) < x1 OR
         points(count,1) > x2 OR
         points(count,2) > y1 OR
         points(count,2) < y2 :
      ('point ' ,l,'not within range',newline);

```
                    points(count,1) >= x1 OR
                    points(count,1) <= x2 OR
                    points(count,2) >= y1 OR
                    points(count,2) <= y2 :
               ('point ' ,l,'within range',newline)
                    }
          WEND
```

In the definition of the domain of the formal parameter 'points', l and u are themselves formal parameters whose values will depend on the size of the structure passed as an actual parameter. It is assumed that the lower bound (l) of the parameter 'points' is increased each time the function 'test if contained' is called. This is not the case in some languages, for example, where the lower bound of an array passed as a parameter is always taken as being 1. If this convention was adopted then an additional count parameter would have to have been used, which would have been incremented for each call of the function.

In [PRe76] the design of a program is carried further, to include the design of the database, and to cover such points as the conversion of the inputs to appropriate units. Such extensions are beyond the scope of this example, but it should be obvious how such extensions could be made.

It is worth illustrating the method by which we would expect the above program to be executed. This would be done by writing:

PRINTER = select within range (FILE.MAP, FILE.POINTS,

CONSOLE)

where PRINTER, FILE, and CONSOLE are system functions with the obvious meanings.

Finally we present an alternative solution to the problem which does not produce a template, but merely examines a given point to see if it is within range. A circular 'template' is used.

```
test a point = [map : {1..4} → INT, point : {1,2} → INT,
               address : {1,2} → INT, radius : INT]
          ('point ' , {withinmap :
                         {withinrange : 'within range' ;
                          NOT withinrange : 'not in range'} ;
                          NOT withinmap : 'not within map'})
          WITH withinmap =
               address(1) >= map(1) AND
               address(1) <= map(2) AND
```

$$\text{address}(2) >= \text{map}(3) \text{ AND}$$
$$\text{address}(2) <= \text{Map}(4),$$
$$\text{withinrange} =$$
$$\text{sqrt}((\text{address}(1) - \text{point}(1)) \uparrow 2 +$$
$$(\text{address}(2) - \text{point}(2)) \uparrow 2) <= \text{radius}$$
$$\text{WEND}$$

We have discussed the methods by which a data flow programming language may be built up from the primitive model presented earlier.

We now turn our attention to some of the alternative data flow programming languages that have been suggested. We shall briefly consider three languages: Id, Val, and Lapse. Rather than present detailed descriptions, we shall give some short example program fragments which will illustrate the basic design philosophies involved.

Id (Irvine dataflow) was developed by Arvind, Gostelow and Plouffe at the University of California at Irvine [AGP78]. It is a block-structured, expression-oriented, single-assignment language. In order to illustrate what is meant by 'expression-oriented', let us consider the following Id program fragment to find the maximum of two values:

$$\text{max} \leftarrow (\text{if } x > y \text{ then } x \text{ else } y)$$

The conditional construct is an expression, not a statement as in conventional languages.

Unlike the language introduced earlier in this chapter, Id provides an iteration facility, but once again this is packaged as an expression rather than as the control construct we are used to. The following program fragment calculates the factorial function iteratively.

```
initial I ← N; J ← 1
while I <> 0
do    new I ← I – 1;
      new J ← J * I;
return J
```

The iteration expression returns a value (as all expressions must), in this case J. The 'body' of the loop contains a series of assignments which must obey the single-assignment rule, and which are carried out in an order determined by data dependencies. In order to implement the iterative nature of a loop the word 'new' is used to distinguish between values of variables on each iteration. The loop expression thus implicitly implies an ordering.

Lapse, designed as part of an M.Sc. project by John Glauert at Manchester University [Gla78], also includes an iterative construct, but uses 'old' to refer to values from a previous iteration rather than 'new'. The factorial example would be written as below:

```
decl n, facn, dummy : integer;
iteration factorial (i, f : integer);
while old i > 1
do {i, f} ← {old i − 1, old i * old f}
od;
begin {dummy, facn} ← factorial(n,1)
end
```

A number of differences are immediately apparent. Firstly loop expressions in Lapse return a value corresponding to each of the values that are passed into the loop initially rather than being able to return only one, which explains the need for the variable dummy.

The assignment {i, f} ← {old i − 1, old i * old f} could in fact be written as two separate assignments, as in the Id example. Id also includes a facility for multiple assignments such as this one. A multiple assignment ensures parallelism, whereas assignments which are written as a set of statements are carried out in parallel only if this is allowed by the data dependencies.

Another difference between the Lapse and Id examples is the type information supplied in the Lapse example. The design of Lapse is strongly influenced by Pascal. If instead of **decl** we had used **var**, then the similarity might be even clearer. The symbol **od** has been used to terminate loops, and **fi** is used to terminate conditional expressions, thus avoiding the need for additional statement brackets to prevent ambiguity in nested conditionals, and many compound statements. An Algol 68 influence can be seen in these modifications.

Type declarations are not included in Id; the argument is that since we only ever assign to a variable once its type can be determined uniquely at that point.

The Pascal typing influence on Lapse can also be seen if we look at structured types. Consider the following program to perform a complex multiplication.

```
type complex = record {re, im : real};
decl x, y, z : complex;
function cmult(a, b : complex) : complex;
begin cmult ← {(a.re * b.re) − (a.im * b.im),
                (a.re * b.im) + (a.im * b.re)}
end;
begin z ← cmult(x, y)
end.
```

Val (A Value-oriented Algorithmic Language) was developed by Jack Dennis's group at MIT [ADe79]. It, too, explicitly defines types, but tends to do so *in situ* rather than at the beginning of a program as in Lapse. We will present the two examples we have looked at earlier in Val.

```
for Y : integer := 1 : P : integer := N;
do  if P <> 1 then iter Y := Y * P; P := P - 1; enditer
    else Y
    endif
endfor
```

```
function cmult(X, Y : complex returns complex)
    type complex = record [re, im : real] ;
    record [re : X.re * Y.re - X.im * Y.im;
            im : X.im * Y.re + X.re * Y.im
           ]
endfun
```

One point to note about the first example is the way in which Val explicitly specifies the piece of code which is to be iterated and avoids the messy use of old or new. **endif** and **endfor** are used in preference to Algol 68's **fi** and **od**.

Val, Lapse and Id are all much closer in syntactic style to conventional languages such as Pascal than the language developed earlier. Val contains some syntax reminiscent of Ada. Although it may be argued that this makes them more acceptable to many programmers, it may be counterproductive in that it discourages them from really understanding what is implied by the new data flow model of computing. We are not arguing for change just for change's sake, rather that new ideas are probably more readily expressed using new notations.

10

Other languages

It has been argued that traditional control flow languages are not particularly suited for use with the data flow model of computing. In this chapter some other languages which are neither data flow nor control flow will be briefly examined and their relationship to the data flow model of computing discussed.

We have already dealt with the best-known functional language, Lisp, in the chapter on control flow languages. As we pointed out then Pure Lisp, since it is a functional language, would be suitable for use with our functional data flow model. However, to many people the current notation is not as readable as it could be. Furthermore the extended Lisp notation used as a programming language, introduces strictly sequential features such as the PROG function, and is less appropriate for use with the data flow approach.

It is perhaps also worth mentioning the ideas presented by Landin for ISWIM [Lan66] which is again to a large extent functionally based, and which introduced the idea of a where clause that is similar to our notion of a qualification clause (WITH..WEND).

An alternative mathematical basis for the development of a programming notation is predicate logic [Kow74]. This is a more user-oriented approach, since predicate logic is derived from efforts to formalise the properties of rational thought. The declarative semantics of the language Prolog (see, for example [WPP77] is based on predicate logic. This allows a Prolog program to be regarded as a set of descriptive statements about a problem. Thus the approach is very much in sympathy with the way in which we have developed our data flow model of computing.

Another method of program definition which seems closely related to our model is the use of recursion equations. Research into various ways of making the implementation of recursion equations more efficient (in some sense) has been done (see, for example [BDa77] and [Sch77]), but it has always been based on the use of traditional control flow machines. In a single-assignment language, such as the one we have developed for our data flow model of computing, statements can be read as equations. Thus it would seem likely that the data flow approach to providing a model of computation should provide a much more satisfactory base for the development of recursion equation languages.

The next language to be discussed is Lucid [AWa77]. Lucid was developed as an aid to the design of correct programs, in the sense that Lucid is both a programming notation and a notation for proving that programs are correct. Although Lucid is not a data flow language some work has been done using data flow techniques to implement it. According to Bill Wadge, one of the designers of Lucid, one of the problems in defining a data flow semantics for Lucid is that the data flow graph produced from a Lucid program may deadlock in the process of computing unnecessary values [Wad78]. This lack of coincidence between the mathematical and the data flow semantics of Lucid can be interpreted in two ways: as evidence that the purely mathematical approach is in some respects unrealistic; or as evidence that data flow is in some respects inadequate. Wadge argues for the latter, but he bases his argument on the classical data flow model rather than on the model presented in this book. If the functional model presented in this book is adopted, then it can be argued that Wadge's case is no longer valid; rather, any remaining inconsistency is a result of Lucid's mathematical semantics being unrealistic. This apparent inconsistency between the data flow model and the mathematical model assumed by Lucid does, however, make the adoption of Lucid as our programming language less attractive.

The functional language FP [Bac78] has already been briefly discussed in Chapter 4. Clearly as a functional notation it would be possible to use FP, or a variation of it, as a data flow programming language.

A final language that is worth mentioning is MIRANDA [Tur84], which is a development of KRC [Tur82], which was itself a development of SASL [Tur76]. Here again we have a functional notation which could be used with the data flow approach. In many ways MIRANDA is much closer to the notation presented in this book than any of the other languages we have mentioned. However, it is important to realise that the model of computing upon which it is based is fundamentally different from the one introduced in this book. This can affect the detailed interpretation of some programs.

11

Languages for data flow: summary

In this part of the book we developed a programming language based on the data flow model of computing introduced earlier. We also looked at a number of other programming languages with a view to seeing if they could also be used with the data flow approach. We saw that the languages which we classified as control flow languages (Fortran, Pascal, etc.) could be used with the data flow model of computing, but since they are based on a fundamentally different model the approach did not seem altogether satisfactory.

Languages which used a functional model as their basis seemed much more appropriate for use with a data flow approach. It could be argued that the data flow model of computing, and purely functional models are really different ways of expressing the same ideas. The importance of the data flow approach is the insight it can give us into how to directly implement the model in a computer and this is the topic we will turn to in the next part of this book.

The other topic discussed in the previous few chapters was the use of graphical notations to represent programs and computations. This approach complements the textual programming language we have developed. A graphical approach can be used as an aid in understanding problems. It may also be helpful in clarifying our ideas on implementation approaches. We will sometimes use the graphical model to illustrate our discussion of implementation methods in the next part of the book.

Part

DATA FLOW ARCHITECTURES AND IMPLEMENTATION TECHNIQUES

12

The Von Neumann machine

In this part of the book it is intended to look at some of the implications of the data flow model of computing for machine design. In the next chapter the nature of programs, and in particular data flow programs, will be reviewed, and some desirable features for a data flow machine will be discussed. Subsequent chapters will discuss more detailed machine designs and implementation techniques. First of all, however, it is probably worthwhile to remind ourselves of how the traditional von Neumann computer works, and also to examine some of the ways in which people have attempted to improve its performance.

We briefly introduced the von Neumann computer in Chapter 2 when we disucssed the control flow model of computing. The design consists of five components:

— an input unit
— an output unit
— a memory unit
— an arithmetic and logic computation unit (ALU)
— a control unit
(the control unit and ALU combined are often referred to as the CPU).

The program is held in memory, and a single sequence control register points at one instruction after another, causing the execution of the instruction currently being pointed at.

There are various ways which have been tried to increase the throughput of a simple von Neumann computer. Essentially all of them require replication of one or more components of the basic architecture. Multiple input/output units are now commonplace making multi-user systems possible. By allowing many users to have interactive access to the machine, an apparent increase in throughput, as perceived by the user, is achieved. Introducing multiple memory units makes parallel memory access possible, thus reducing the bottleneck caused by the need to transfer all data and instructions between the CPU and the memory.

Using faster components at the von Neumann bottleneck can obviously give us an increase in speed. It turns out, however, that in order to achieve any meaningful speed-up it is necessary to duplicate at least part of the CPU. The obvious approach is to replicate the whole processor, including some internal memory. The problem with these multiprocessors is the communication required between them in order to synchronise the computation. Sometimes the whole program is duplicated in the memory of each processor. This seemingly wasteful use of memory capacity is usually justified by the savings achieved from not having to transfer program segments around during execution.

One way of reducing the problems inherent in a full multiprocessor system is to limit the potential for parallelism by replicating only part of the CPU. A classic example of this approach is the array processor, where the ALU is replicated, but only one control unit is used. The many problems which require the same operation to be performed on many items of data can be speeded up in this way. This approach is not as limiting as might appear at first because, given the possibility of performing a single operation on many items of data (an array of data) at once, many problems can be recast in terms of array operations to utilise the parallelism provided (see, for example, [Par82]).

Another approach, which again duplicates ALUs but keeps a single control unit, is the multi-function processor, where extra, specialised ALUs are added. For example, multiple floating point adders could be provided to allow floating point calculations to be overlapped. Special units to perform character manipulation could be provided. An increase in throughput is achieved both by having multiple ALUs to perform operations in parallel and by having special-purpose ALUs which can be designed so as to perform some complex operations faster than a traditional general-purpose ALU.

In order to achieve any speed-up, some overlapping of computation is clearly required. The pipeline processor is the ultimate in achieving speed-up by overlapping. The traditional instruction cycle consists of five phases:

— transfer address in SCR to memory unit
— read from that address to control unit (op-code) and ALU (operand)
— decode the instruction
— instruct the ALU to perform the operation
— set the SCR to next instruction.

In the pipeline processor these operations are overlapped. As soon as one instruction has been read, the next one is fetched, and decoded, so that as soon as the ALU has finished one operation it can immediately start the next without waiting for the control unit to do its work. Parallel reading and writing of the memory unit is also necessary to utilise this approach fully. The only replication needed is the partial replication of the control unit. The concept fails if the next instruction required is in fact not the next one in sequence — that is, if a jump instruction is performed.

We now return to the full multiprocessor solution, where the whole CPU is replicated. The synchronisation problem, and hence the communication problem, is partly caused by the control flow nature of conventional languages. One control path is completely specified, and all the CPUs have to refer to this path. Specific parallel operations have to be defined in order to achieve parallel computation and, if the physical number of processors differs from the abstract number assumed, the allocation of tasks can become a serious problem.

The data flow approach to some extent alleviates this problem by allowing individual parts of a program (single operations) to control the order of execution either by the availability of data or by the need for data. The remaining problem in data flow multiprocessors is therefore the need to pass large amounts of information between components of the system.

In any program many data values are used only with a strictly limited part of the whole program. With high-level languages this is emphasised by the use of local variables in procedures or modules. Unless this locality of data in programs can be successfully exploited in the architecture the need to pass large amounts of data between components of the system is likely to remain a limiting factor in data flow computer design.

13

The relationship between implementation and machine architecture

In [Bir76] it was proved that for all **while** programs (iterative programs) there is a strongly equivalent recursive program, and that the converse is not true. On the other hand, in [BJa66] it is shown that iteration and composition are sufficient for the specification of all programs. Thus, although for every recursive program there need not be a strongly equivalent iterative program, there must exist a weakly equivalent one (in some sense).

Therefore in any programming language we have a choice between representing recursive programs or iterative programs. It is our contention that recursive programs are more natural and easier to program with [Sha82]. (Remember that a truly iterative program forbids any recursive constructs unless you build them yourself, as in Fortran.)

The same distinction can be drawn in data flow programs. To illustrate the concepts involved, a graphical notation will be assumed, but the same arguments apply to textual notations.

An iterative program can, in some sense, be regarded as being evaluated in a **static** manner, in that all possible nodes and arcs (in a graphical representation) can be drawn out before execution begins. We shall, of course, have to include nodes to add labels to, and check labels on, data tokens, to ensure that all values are matched correctly in the cyclic constructs. This is necessary to avoid the problem of race conditions which we discussed earlier.

A recursive program can be regarded as being evaluated in a **dynamic** manner, since we must regard the recursive definitions as being 'expanded' at run-time.

If we had chosen to use only iterative programs, we would clearly need only a static evaluation mechanism. Having chosen to adopt recursive programs, we have a choice:

Either (1) to have a static evaluation mechanism (and compile all recursive programs into iterative equivalents — a non-trivial task),

or (2) to have a dynamic evaluation mechanism.

Three basic types of architectures for implementing data flow programs will now be defined.

(a) *Static architecture*

This type is not really very interesting, since a truly static architecture can evaluate only one program graph. Possibly the only interesting static architecture would be one which could evaluate the program which could run any program (i.e. the interpreter). In this case we would be transferring all the complexity of executing a data flow program away from the architecture design to the compilation stage. This may be acceptable as an alternative strategy. If we adopted this approach, however, it is difficult to see how we would decide what form the machine architecture should take. It is clearly possible to implement a data flow language on a conventional von Neumann machine, but this would not seem to be a very attractive approach to take. For the purposes of this book we will concentrate on the possibility of designing an architecture to reflect the nature of a data flow program.

(b) *Reconfigurable static architecture*

This means a machine (consisting of a number of processors) where the logical interconnections between the processors are made when the program is loaded. This implies that decisions about what connections are needed are made by the compiler and/or the loader and remain fixed throughout execution. This approach would seem to suggest that,

(1) most possible physical connections must exist, and
(2) the number of processors available must be in excess of the minimum necessary, since it is difficult to see how optimal re-use of processors is possible with fixed links.

(c) *Dynamic architecture*

This architecture is by far the most interesting one, since it is the only type that allows us to evaluate programs dynamically. The other two types allow us to evaluate them only statically. The main feature of a dynamic architecture is that the logical connections between processors can be changed during the execution of a program.

Logical structure

It was stated at the start of this chapter that the aim was to try to identify some architectural features that may be considered as fundamental in the design of a data flow machine. As a first step, let us try to identify the logical structure of the machine that data flow implies. We shall restrict our attention to a dynamic architecture.

Looking at modern program design techniques (see, for example, [Wir71]) we see that the resulting programs tend to have a hierarchical structure. This is true also of data flow programs, where initially abstract/complex operations at nodes can be refined by graphs (programs) constructed of simpler nodes (operations).

Drawing a diagram of the logical structure would yield a tree. Control flows from the roots to the leaves, and results flow back from the leaves to the roots. This rather simplified view leads one to suggest that the logical connections between processors in a data flow machine should be representable as a tree. Davis's DDM1 machine is such a design [Dav78].

Physical structure

An obvious architecture would seem to be a physical representation of the logical tree structure, such as DDM1. A moment's thought, however, should show that such an architecture would require many more processors than the minimum number required for any particular computation, and that it would be difficult (if not impossible) to ensure that all possible parallelism would be exploited. After all, the tree structure would be static, and we have said that we need a dynamic architecture. A partially dynamic tree architecture designed to execute Lisp programs has been proposed by Patil *et al.* in [PKL78]. This design will be discussed further in Chapter 15.

We reject a simple tree design for a data flow machine for the reasons explained above.

Another obvious design is one in which all processors may communicate directly with all others. It is perfectly possible to envisage such a machine if we have only a small number of processors. For example a machine consisting of four processors would require six connection paths in order for each processor to be directly connected to every other one. The number of connections required for n processors is the factorial of (n−1). This means that for a machine of eight processors the number of connection paths rises to twenty-eight and if we were talking about machines with tens of hundreds of processors then clearly the number of connections required would be physically impossible to realise efficiently.

Clearly the problem of transmitting data and/or instructions between the component processors in a multiprocessor data flow machine is going to be one of the major concerns in any design. A parallel may be drawn with the von Neumann machine where one way in which the efficiency of the execution process can be increased is by keeping commonly used values within registers in the central processing unit rather than performing repeated store and fetch instructions which involve transmitting data between the memory and the CPU. Values which are used only within a limited number of adjacent instructions may be considered local to that piece of code. Such local items of data would ideally be kept within the CPU and would not be repeatedly swapped in and out of memory. Similarly within a data flow program it may be possible to detect values which are used by only a limited number of instructions. Such locality of use might be exploited by keeping those values within a given processor. This would reduce the amount of information which would have to be passed between processors, and thus reduce the communication problem.

Let us now summarise the sorts of features we would expect to find in a data flow computer.

(a) There should be some form of dynamic linking. Every individual processor should be able to initiate requests for links, and it should not be necessary for the linking process to involve a central processor or group of processors, since this could produce a bottleneck.

(b) As explained above some way of exploiting the locality of values which occurs in most programs is surely necessary in order to avoid excessive communication overheads. It may be possible to do this by using some form of hierarchical structure which reflects the typical program structure resulting from the use of modern top-down design techniques.

(c) A design with the above features would preferably be constructed from a limited number of component types (ideally just one). These components should be as simple as possible.

14

Data flow implementation strategies

A data flow model of computation has been presented and the principles behind the design of a high-level programming language discussed.

The model of computation is theoretically neat, and concise; the machine architecture ideas are, however, still open to discussion (see [Sha80]). In this chapter it is intended to discuss some of the aspects of the theoretical model which are not, perhaps, ideally suited to efficient implementation, and to present some ideas on how a more efficient implementation might be achieved. If we use a naive approach to implementation based on the theoretical model presented an excessive amount of memory space seems to be required. It is this kind of 'inefficiency' which many people seem to regard as inevitable in a data flow implementation, and which we intend to show is not inevitable.

Push v. Pull
Within the data flow model of computing there are two basic approaches to evaluation — either the demand-driven approach, where data is **pulled** towards the output as it is needed, or the data-driven approach, in which the arrival of data **pushes** information towards the output stage.

. To the high-level language programmer, whether a push or a pull method of evaluation is used should make no difference; it was seen

earlier, however, that in a graphical notation it is not so straightforward at a low level if we wish to avoid impossible computations.
It is definitely the case that the operational semantics would be very
different if a push model of evaluation was chosen rather than a pull.
It is improbable that the mathematical semantics would be dependent upon the decision, though there is no proof of this.

The language presented in this book bears a close relation to
lambda calculus. Various machines have been proposed for evaluating
lambda expressions (see, for example, [Lan64]). The conditions for
termination are not always the same, and proving that they are for
two different machines is a non-trivial task.

Similarly proving the equivalence of the push and pull methods
of evaluation for data flow is, in the general case, a non-trivial task.
For the general case it will be undecidable, as with any conventional
model of computation. For the purposes of this book, however, the
adoption of either the push or pull method of evaluation (or even a
hybrid method) will be regarded as an implementation decision
which depends upon the machine architecture chosen. (It is assumed
that efficiency is a machine-dependent feature, since if a machine has
a large number of processors it is not necessarily inefficient to use
some of them on potentially useless tasks.)

Sufficient input sets

In the model introduced in Chapter 3 it was assumed that all inputs
must be present for a function to be evaluated. Clearly even at the
lowest nor gate level this restriction is not strictly essential (if one
input is TRUE then the output must be FALSE, and the other input
is unnecessary). Relaxing the restriction would lead to a significant
increase in throughput, by preventing unnecessary delay in waiting
for an unwanted result, but two points must be borne in mind.

(a) Although an input may no longer be required it is still likely to
be produced, thus reducing the theoretical savings possible.
Furthermore any system of halting unnecessary computation
could lead to a large amount of additional control computation,
again negating the possible savings gained by relaxing the conditions on inputs.

(b) Some programs will terminate that otherwise would not, because
the (now) unnecessary result may be impossible to calculate. It
could be argued, depending upon your viewpoint, that this is
either an advantage or a disadvantage. Perhaps the best answer
would be for the relaxation of input restrictions at a low level to
be a user option.

Stream-like implementation

The possibility of a stream-like method of implementation of functions is discussed by Burge in [Bur75], from which we quote:

> When one function produces a list in its natural order and another processes the list of items in the same order, it is often unnecessary to produce the whole list before applying the second function to it.
>
> It is often easier to write programs in two stages in which the list is an intermediate result of the computation. However, it is more economical in storage to use the combination of the two functions in which only one member of the list appears as an intermediate result.

In presenting the model there was no need to distinguish stream functions, and, as Burge says, it is often more natural not to use stream functions. Stream-like functions can always be defined if so desired. (It is possible to envisage the sorting functions of Chapter 9 as acting upon streams.) It is going to be desirable for functions to be evaluated before all the input is available (i.e. in a stream-like manner) – particularly in the case of input/output. Clearly the two points we have just mentioned need to be borne in mind. One further point must be considered in connection with input and output. Theoretically a program could reference the whole of its input (or output) at once. Since the input (output) may take the physical form of a long magnetic tape, or other serial device, such access is practically impossible. It is therefore necessary to allow functions to be evaluated with partial inputs, and produce partial outputs. Functions may thus be considered to be evaluated in a stream-like manner, though this is invisible to the user. More visible to the user is the need to restrict the extent of the input (output) function which is accessible at any time. Some form of limited size random access buffer is required for access to the physical serial access device. The size of this buffer could be variable, according to resource availability and options selected by the user. An optimising implementation could, perhaps, determine the maximum size required for the buffer.

The term 'compiler' is avoided since, although parallel compilation techniques for multiprocessors have been studied (see, for example, [Sch79]), it is felt that the ideal approach to an implementation may be closer to a cross between an interpreter and a compiler. In particular it is unclear at what stage in the implementation process it would be possible, for example, to allocate tasks to processors, decide when to expand the code for function calls, or decide how many copies of a recursive function to allow to be evaluated in parallel. The use of the term 'compiler' might be taken to imply that most, if not all, such decisions should be made before execution starts, and that some form of machine code version of a program can be loaded into the memories of the various processors within a data flow machine. The term interpreter, on the other hand, might seem to imply the adoption of the opposite philosophy of delaying all such decisions until a particular function, or piece of code needs to be evaluated. The author feels that an approach somewhere in between these two extremes would be best. That is, some of the decisions on the allocation of code and the expansion of function definitions would be made prior to execution, and some would be left to be made dynamically during execution. Some way of anticipating, for example, what functions would need to be expanded in the near future would be a useful way of improving the performance of such a dynamic implementation strategy.

Discarding useless information
Recursion generally implies retaining on a stack a basic 'frame' of information for each function invocation. In tail recursion, where the recursive call is the last instruction to be evaluated in the function, much of the information stored is unnecessary. Only the return address is required since no further work is done once control is returned from the recursive call. Therefore tail recursion need not involve any more overhead than conventional iteration. With a non-procedural language it is possible for some computation to be carried on in parallel to the recursive call. If evaluation within the calling function is completed before the recursive call, then the information stored on the stack can again be reduced to just the return address. By discarding useless nested information from recursive calls a non-procedural recursive program, of the type described above, may be evaluated repeatedly without any form of stack overflow. In this manner a program may be run continuously, thus making real-time programming possible.

The avoidance of unnecessary evaluation
Each definition of a function case provides a method of evaluating a set of more specific function cases. For example the following case from a factorial function definition:

$$\text{fact} = [a : a > 1] \; a * \text{fact}(a-1)$$

may be regarded as including the specific cases:

$$\text{fact} = [a : 4] \; 24,$$
$$\text{fact} = [a : 5] \; 120,$$
$$\text{fact} = [a : 2] \; 2$$
$$\text{and others.}$$

If a specific case (e.g. fact(5)) is required many times in a program, it would be desirable to avoid re-evaluating that function case.

Every time a specific function case is evaluated, that specific case is added to the definition (equivalently, a guard is added to a guarded expression list).

Because of the single-assignment rule, no incorrect evaluation in subsequent references is possible.

Clearly there is a limit to the number of cases that can be remembered. This limit would be dependent on resource availability. When too many cases are added the least used cases would have to be deleted (excluding, of course, the original definition cases).

Determinism and definition by cases

To achieve determinism we have assumed that each case in a function definition should be mutually exclusive. It should be possible to define a nondeterminate semantics, but since we have no experience of utilising nondeterminism it seems inappropriate to define a nondeterminate semantics at the moment.

One problem remains, namely checking the determinism of the program. With the full generality of case definition which we have allowed this is a run-time problem which would certainly involve a large amount of computation, and is undecidable in the general case.

Conclusions

In this chapter we have considered some of the decisions that have to be made by anyone who wishes to implement a data flow programming system. We cannot say which is the best approach until much more work has been done in this area. Even then it is improbable that any one approach will be the best in all cases. What we can do is to indicate which ways seem most likely to yield a reasonably efficient implementation. What is meant by the concept of efficiency is, of course, open to discussion. Without being too precise let us assume it means developing an implementation which will execute most programs without too much waste of resource (human or machine) in a reasonable amount of time.

It seems likely that any implementation would be a hybrid demand/data-driven one. A pure demand-driven system may cause evaluation to be delayed unnecessarily, whereas a pure data-driven system seems to give rise to the possibility of performing a great deal of unnecessary work. Some element of demand-driven evaluation seems essential to control the evaluation process, yet, once started, data-driven evaluation has attractions as far as speed is concerned. At a high level, evaluation of a function should occur as soon as any input is available, but it would seem unreasonable to extend this philosophy to machine level (and below?).

With respect to recursion, and repeated evaluation of function cases a major problem is that of code copying and expansion. It is necessary to find an approach which can permit a large amount of parallel evaluation but which has a reasonable space requirement.

As far as determinism is concerned it would seem unreasonable to make the writing of nondeterministic programs impossible, though at the moment it is not at all clear how useful they might be. On the other hand it is obvious that programmers must be given some way of preventing unwanted nondeterminism. One possible solution would be for guarded expression lists to be determinate, and for function cases to be allowed to introduce nondeterminism.

15

Data flow architectures

The main aim of this chapter is not to present the ideal design for a data flow architecture, but rather to consider some of the designs that have been proposed and point out their limitations. At the end of the chapter an alternative design will be presented which, in the author's opinion, would overcome some of these limitations.

In Chapter 13 we identified some of the features that we would expect to find in any data flow architecture. Bearing these conclusions in mind we shall briefly look at the two basic types of dynamic architecture that have been proposed — rings and networks.

Ring architectures

In a ring architecture there are many processors, each producing results. These are returned to a memory/control unit which collects together the results required by subsequent operations and generates new tasks (operations and required inputs) which are passed around the ring. A simple ring is shown in Fig. 15.1.

A number of rings may be connected together in parallel layers with a switch allowing communication between the rings. In such an architecture the control function may be distributed between the different layers, but we still have a logical cyclic construction with a separation of the control and execution tasks.

A typical ring architecture is the design of Gurd and Watson which is currently being built at Manchester University [GWa80]. Fig. 15.2 illustrates the basic design of their machine. Results will be produced by the processing units at different rates at different stages of execution, depending upon the number, and complexity, of the operations currently being performed. At certain times results may be produced faster than the matching store can process them. The result queue is a way of temporarily storing such results.

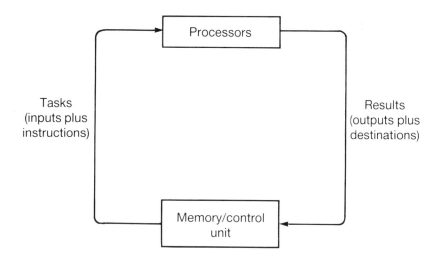

Fig. 15.1 — A simple ring architecture.

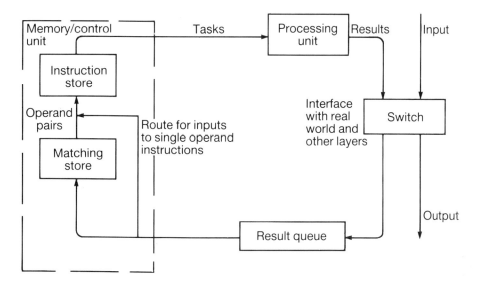

Fig. 15.2 — The Manchester data flow architecture.

Network architectures

A network architecture will often physically resemble a ring architecture, but the control task is now carried out by the processors, and not by a separate control unit. A simple network architecture is shown in Fig. 15.3. The elementary MIT data flow processor described by Misunas in [Mis78] is an example of a network architecture.

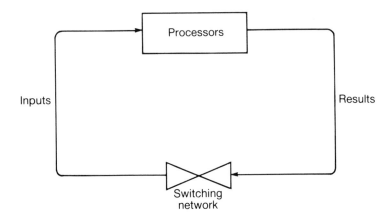

Fig. 15.3 — A simple network architecture.

We mentioned earlier that in any program some data values are only required to be accessible within a limited part of the program. Exploiting such locality of reference could help to reduce the communication overhead inherent in any dynamic architecture consisting of a number of interconnected processors. In a network architecture locality can be introduced by having layers, as in a ring architecture, or by arranging a network of processor groups as shown in Fig. 15.4.

An obvious architecture would seem to be a physical representation of the logical tree structure, such as the DDM1 design proposed by Davis [Dav78]. As we mentioned before though, such an architecture would require many more processors than the minimum number required for any given computation. Furthermore it would be difficult (if not impossible) to ensure that all possible parallelism would be exploited. After all the tree structure would be static, and we have said that we need a dynamic architecture. Patil, Keller and Lindstrom of Utah presented a design for a partially dynamic tree architecture in [PKL78] (see Fig. 15.5). This machine was designed to execute Lisp programs and as such is not a true data flow machine. Nevertheless it can be viewed as one if we consider the arbiter and distributer units as performing the same task as the matching store

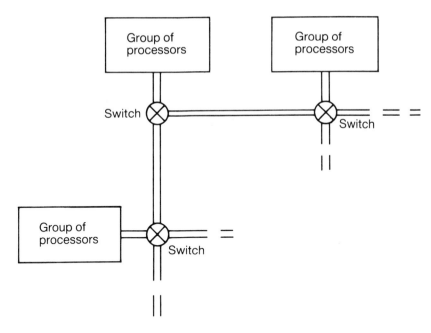

Fig. 15.4 — A network of groups of processors.

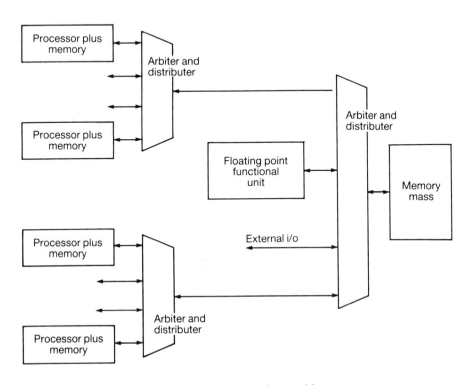

Fig. 15.5 — The Utah Lisp machine.

in the Manchester design. Locality can theoretically be exploited by restricting the use of values to processors controlled by the same arbiter and distributer unit.

This design seems to involve a number of distinct types of component (processors, arbiter and distributer units, memory mass, specialised arithmetic units) and thus in some ways seems less attractive than the simple network approach which consists only of switches and processors. Furthermore the hierarchical tree structure still seems rather rigid. It may be argued that typical Lisp programs fit more naturally than general data flow programs on to such a structure, but we ought to consider if there are any alternatives.

In Chapter 13 we also mentioned the obvious design in which all processors may communicate directly with all others. We rejected this design as being physically impossible to realise efficiently.

Let us return to the idea of a truly dynamic architecture which seems to imply the adoption of either a ring or a network structure.

The two forms of communication required between processors are:

(1) delegation of tasks, and
(2) returning results.

The simple structure shown in Fig. 15.6 could be offered as a solution. This structure has no hierarchy, however, and we have said that a logical tree structure such as the one shown in Fig. 15.7 would be desirable. The horizontal links would make it possible to reconfigure the tree in order to allow for unbalanced hierarchies. The structure shown is basically a binary tree; an n-ary tree is more likely to be required — but what value should n have?

The earlier simple design could be adapted to introduce the notion of hierarchy into the architecture as shown in Fig. 15.8. Input to the machine would be in the form of tasks at the 'highest' level, and results from this level would form the output. It would be expected that the higher rings would require fewer processors, and that at lower levels it may be possible to utilise parallel rings. Multiple processors at the top level would make it possible to implement a multiprogramming system. Multiprogramming may have the advantage of reducing the amount of unbalanced (tree-wise) processing that needs to be done. Multiprogramming various unbalanced programs should lead to a balanced average workload.

It should be noted that the architecture described above entails processors waiting for results rather than allowing them to carry on executing other tasks. This may be reasonable if we ensure that, whenever a processor delegates a task or tasks, it always retains the longest one to execute itself. Detecting which task is going to be the longest may not always be possible, however, so it could be argued that the results switch ought to be replaced by a queue similar to that used for tasks. If this is done, is there any difference between tasks and results, and have we really gained anything?

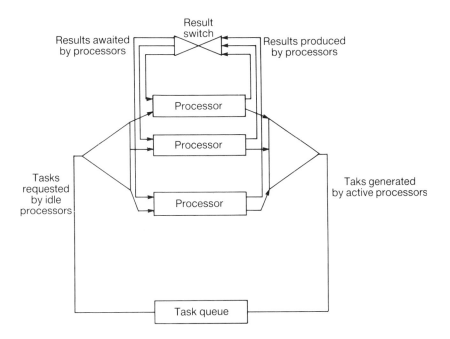

Fig. 15.6 — A simple dynamic data flow architecture.

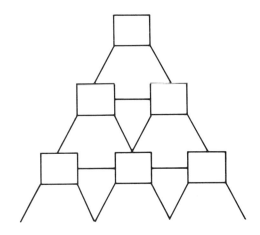

Fig. 15.7 — A hierarchical structure for a data flow machine.

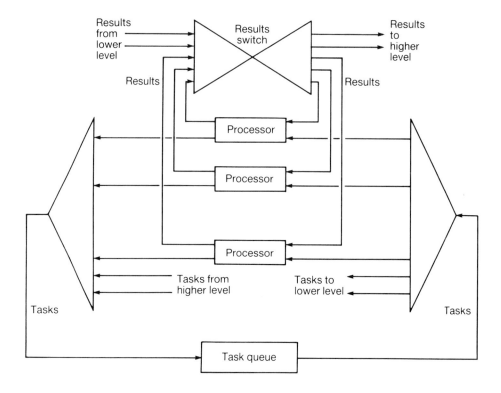

Fig. 15.8 — A dynamic hierarchical data flow architecture.

In this chapter we have attempted to examine some of the alternative data flow machine architectures that have been proposed. As yet it remains unclear which approach (if any) of those discussed will yield the best results.

16

Reduction machines

So far we have considered the ways in which conventional machines may be modified to increase throughput, and the way in which machines can be designed using data flow principles. We noted in the discussion of the data flow model of computing its close relationship with the functional approach. In this chapter we shall briefly examine two ways that have been proposed for implementing functional programs in hardware. Both are based on the concept of reduction.

In simple terms, reduction means replacing part of the original source code by its meaning. For example if one expression in the program is '2 * 3' then it can be reduced to '6'.

This implies that reduction takes place by string replacement. This type of reduction is called 'string reduction'. There is an alternative approach which uses a graphical representation of the code, and pointers are manipulated rather than code being copied. This is known as 'graph reduction'.

The first machine design we shall consider is one that uses string reduction. It is a tree-based design developed by Gyula Mago of Chapel Hill, North Carolina [Mag80]. The design is based on using large numbers of relatively simple components, and is intended to be ideal for VLSI. The basic interconnection of cells is shown in Fig. 16.1. The horizontal connections between the leaves can, according to Mago, be omitted without impairing the machine's capabilities.

Fig. 16.2 shows how the tree structure can be laid out on a chip using VLSI. This design is easily extensible.

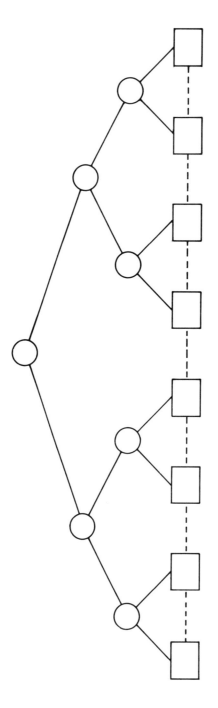

Fig. 16.1 — Basic interconnection structure of Mago's machine.

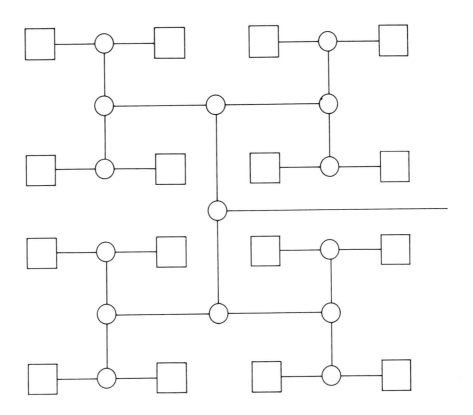

Fig. 16.2 — A possible layout scheme for VLSI.

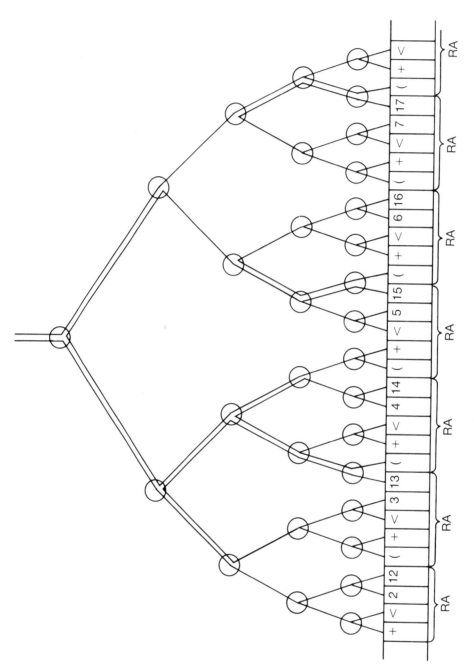

Fig. 16.3 — Part of the tree with code at leaves.

The program to be evaluated is an FFP program [Bac78], and is placed directly into the leaf cells. This implies that either the tree must be large enough to contain the whole program, or that only parts of the program are evaluated at once. An example is given in Fig. 16.3. The innermost applications are grouped together as reducible applications (or RAs). Each RA is contained within a separate tree and can be reduced independently, giving a new set of leaves which are grouped into RAs. The process is then repeated until eventually only one RA remains which reduces to the result required. Fig. 16.4 shows some example steps.

initial expression :(⟨AA,+⟩ : ⟨1,11⟩,⟨2,12⟩,⟨3,13⟩,⟨4,14⟩)
AA means Apply to All

step 1 – remove redundant closing ⟩
       and rewrite (with ⟨
           :⟨⟨AA,+ :⟨1,11 ,⟨2,12 ,⟨3,13 ,⟨4,14)

step 2 – rewrite ⟨ with (
           :⟨(AA,+ :⟨1,11 ,⟨2,12 ,⟨3,13 ,⟨4,14)

step 3 – erase AA and mark '+'
         :⟨(+ :⟨1,11 ,⟨2,12 ,⟨3,13 ,⟨4,14)

step 4 – erase leftmost symbol and
       insert the string (+ : on left
       of <   : ⟨(+ :⟨1,11 (+ :⟨2,12 (+ :⟨3,13 (+ :⟨4,14)

step 5 – perform addition
        : ⟨(12, 14, 16, 18)

Fig. 16.4 – Stages in the reduction process for Apply to All.

One problem of the string reduction approach used here is the need to reevaluate common sub-expressions. A graph reduction approach avoids this problem. One design that uses graph reduction is the Alice design proposed by Darlington and Reeve of Imperial College, London [DRe81].

Let us first clarify the difference between graph reduction and string reduction. Consider the definition below:

$$a = (b+c)*(b-c)$$

In string reduction a request for the value of a would result in a copy of the definition '(b+c)*(b−c)' being taken. Then a value of b would be requested giving say

$$(4+c)*(b-c)$$

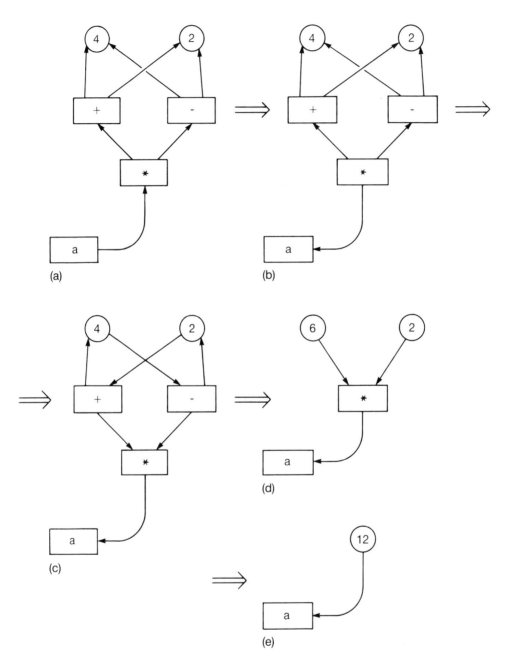

Fig. 16.5 – Example of graph reduction. (a) Initial graph. (b) A request for 'a' reverses the link between 'a' and its definition. (c) Eventually all the arcs are reversed. (d) The first stage of the evaluation. (e) The result is produced.

Evaluation would proceed with the string being rewritten through the following steps

$$(4+2)*(b-c)$$
$$6*(b-c)$$
$$6*(4-c)$$
$$6*(4-2)$$
$$6*2$$
$$12$$

The two brackets could be evaluated in parallel but the values of b and c would be copied twice.

If the same problem were to be evaluated using graph reduction, the point at which a was requested would be given a pointer to the definition. This arc would be traversed (and reversed to allow for a value to be returned). Eventually all the arcs would have been traversed and reversed. Values would then be returned down the arcs, eventually arriving back at the point of the original request. This process is illustrated in Fig. 16.5. The point to note is that if the definition of b had itself been a complex expression, in the string reduction example it would have been evaluated twice, whereas in the graph reduction example it would only need to be evaluated once.

Turning now to the Alice machine, operations (nodes in the graph) are represented by packets. The above example would be represented by the packets shown in Fig. 16.6. Evaluation proceeds by a number of processors each selecting packets which are ready

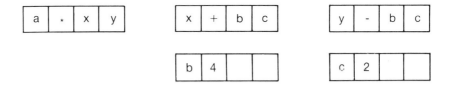

Fig. 16.6 — Alice packets to represent the computation a = (b+c)*(b−c) where b = 4 and c = 2.

to be evaluated (or reduced), performing the appropriate operations, and returning the packets to a pool. A slotted ring is used to allow the individual processors to communicate and select packets (see Fig. 16.7).

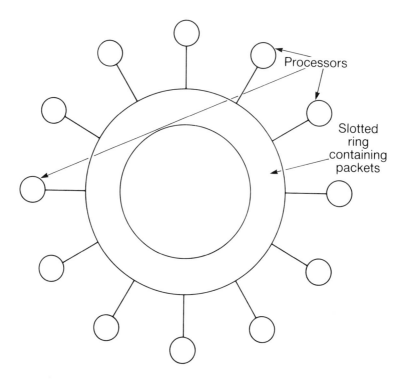

Fig. 16.7 — Slotted ring architecture of the Alice machine.

Both these machine designs may be considered to be data flow designs since they both use the need for data and the availability of data to control the evaluation process. They have, however, been designed primarily as machines to implement applicative languages. Mago's machine is specifically designed to implement Backus's FFP, and it is not easy to see how it could be adopted to implement any other type of language. One advantage of this approach is that there is no need for a compiler. Alice, on the other hand, is a more general design that could be used as a true data flow machine, and any of the data flow languages discussed in this book would be implementable on Alice.

17

Data flow architectures and implementation techniques: summary

The main aim of this part of the book was not to present yet another data flow architecture, but rather to see what features we might expect to find in a data flow architecture and compare them with some of the designs that have been proposed. We have also briefly looked at other machine designs which were not developed using the data flow model as a basis, but are of relevance in the study of data flow computing. None of the architectures presented in Chapter 15 seem particularly attractive, but there seems to be no way of avoiding some form of switching mechanism if we want a dynamic architecture.

If the architectures presented so far do not include the ideal data flow architecture (which is certainly the author's opinion) then what may we expect to see in the ideal design? We summarised some of the main features in Chapter 13:

(a) dynamic linking, controlled by individual processors;
(b) locality probably provided by a hierarchical structure;
(c) a limited number of simple component types (ideally just one).

One problem that most of the architectures we have looked at suffer from is the need to transmit large amounts of control information along with the data so that intermediate results may be combined correctly. As an example the Manchester design uses ninety-six bit words, but only thirty-two bits are used to represent the data value. The other sixty-four bits are used for labels which allow the data values to be collected together in the matching store.

One reason for this problem is that the architectures tend not to exploit locality efficiently. One possible way of overcoming this would be to find paths through program graphs (i.e. sequential sets of nodes), and assign these to processors. By doing this it may be possible to reduce the movement of information by retaining a data value within the individual processor, in much the same way as values are retained within registers in conventional machines.

Another rather more fanciful possibility is the implementation of data flow graphs directly in hardware. It is believed to be possible to specify one function which combines all the primitive functions required, by having sufficient inputs and outputs. An integrated circuit could be made which consisted of hundreds or thousands of these functions, upon which connections could be 'programmed' electronically.

The design of a data flow machine remains an unsolved problem. Nevertheless the use of data flow programming techniques allows us to utilise both the concurrency that exists in programs, and the locality (by finding paths). The approach has, therefore, many advantages over the conventional, sequential control flow approach when considering possible developments for parallel processing.

Part

IV

DATA FLOW
PROGRAMMING
SYSTEMS

18

Introduction

In the first part of this book an abstract data flow model of computing was presented. In the second part a programming notation based on this model was given, and in the third part we discussed the implementation of data flow languages on real computers. Any computer must not only be able to execute programs written in a given language, but must also control the operation of various peripheral devices. In virtually all machines it is the case that more than one program is running simultaneously. The coordination of these tasks is the function of an operating system. In this final part of the book the aim is to see what implications the data flow approach has for the operating systems aspect of computers. It is not intended to show how conventional operating systems may be written in a data flow language. Rather, the topic for discussion is what is meant by an operating system on a data flow machine. We shall examine this subject further in the next chapter.

One aspect of data flow which relates to the operating system is the use of files and input/output. This is the topic discussed in Chapter 20.

Chapter 21 outlines one possible user interface for a data flow machine, assuming that the user is writing programs in a data flow notation.

19

A data flow operating system

Any programming language is usually used in the context of an operating system. In this chapter we will discuss what is meant by an operating system in data flow terms.

Three of the main functions of an operating system in a conventional system may be considered to be:

(a) to control the operation of shared peripheral devices;
(b) to schedule the execution of different user programs within a multi-user environment;
(c) to provide security for user and system files.

Let us now examine the relevance of these functions in a data flow system. The control of shared peripherals is clearly still necessary, as is the maintenance of file security. These functions will be carried out in much the same way as in a conventional system. The question is, how can such functions be expressed in data flow terms? It is to be hoped that the data flow languages that have been developed will enable such operating systems functions to be defined. One drawback to the data flow approach might appear to be the loss of sequentiality, for, without some notion of sequence and time, the allocation of shared resources in a fair manner becomes a problem.

The actual allocation of resources need not be a problem, since we can simply allocate a resource, nondeterministically, to one of the tasks requesting it. What we need to do to ensure fairness is to provide some form of ordering. This can be done by constructing a list, which will be represented in functional terms as we have illustrated for arrays.

We still have not solved all the problems that might arise in developing operating systems in data flow languages. One feature of the data flow approach is that the execution of programs is controlled either by the need for or the availability of data. Most models allow for multiple copies of functions to be evaluated in parallel, in order to achieve maximum speed of execution. If a function is designed to control a given peripheral device, then clearly only one copy of that function can be allowed to be instantiated. Thus we have a need for an extension to the data flow notation to permit the suppression of multiple copies of a function.

The language Id developed at Irvine [AGP78] includes what it terms 'resource managers', which are language features specially designed to cope with this problem. The outline definition below defines a simple resource manager mdl:

$$
\begin{aligned}
&\text{mdl} \leftarrow \textbf{manager} \ (\ S0\ ) \\
&\qquad (\ \textbf{entry}\ X\ \textbf{do} \\
&\qquad\qquad \text{RESULT} \leftarrow (\ \textbf{initial}\ s \leftarrow S0 \\
&\qquad\qquad\qquad\qquad \textbf{for each}\ x\ \text{in}\ X\ \textbf{do} \\
&\qquad\qquad\qquad\qquad\qquad \langle\textbf{new}\ s, \text{answer}\rangle \leftarrow f(s,x) \\
&\qquad\qquad\qquad\qquad \textbf{return all}\ \text{answer} \\
&\qquad\qquad\qquad\qquad) \\
&\qquad\qquad \textbf{exit}\ \text{RESULT} \\
&\qquad)
\end{aligned}
$$

Managers are created with a creation time parameter:

$$m \leftarrow create(mdl,a)$$

To use a manager, a programmer sends an input value to it:

$$z \leftarrow use(m,y)$$

and the result (z) returned is part of a stream of values (X) controlled by the manager. Thus if many programs 'use' a manager m, their respective ys are collected, in a nondeterministic fashion, into a stream of objects, thus controlling the order of use of some resource.

The second function of an operating system was the scheduling of distinct programs from various users. Data flow programs control their own execution order, and the individual operations within a program are executed on one of a number of processors. Thus in a data flow machine scheduling within a program is performed automatically by the processors. Assuming that there are sufficient processors in the machine, multiprogramming can be achieved by running all the programs together, and allowing free processors to select any executable operation from a pool of operations consisting of all the operations from all the currently executing programs.

There are two potential problems with this over-simplified approach. Firstly, one program could theoretically grab all the available processors, effectively locking out all the other programs. A simple solution would be to allocate priorities to executable tasks depending on how long they had been waiting. Essentially the scheduling aspect of the operating system is shifted from the program or job level, down to a lower operation level. It is therefore important to use only a simple scheduling algorithm in this case since the overhead of scheduling will be larger in comparison with the execution times of these short operations.

If a sophisticated scheduling algorithm is required, then the chances are that the machine will have insufficient resources to support the number of programs being executed, and the best that one could hope for would be that the system would degrade into a collection of sequential processors each executing one task, in a relatively inefficient manner. In the worst case an overloaded data flow processor would spend most of its time assigning a series of individual operations from one single program on to many different processors and collecting the results ready to send to other processors. This would result in an excessive amount of inter-processor communication.

The second problem associated with the pool of operations approach is closely related to the third function of an operating system, namely security. There must be a way of ensuring that individual operations from one program cannot interfere with operations from another program. Thus a labelling system for operations is required that unambiguously identifies which job/program it belongs to. Similarly, labels giving access rights to files for different jobs are required to maintain security.

Many of the problems of security, and indeed many of the problems of operating systems, are related to the nature of the devices which the system controls. The processing component of a system is perhaps the easiest component for the operating system to handle. In a data flow system only the processing component has significantly changed. We still have the same form of disk and tape drives as in a conventional system. The terminals connected to the system still have the same characteristics. It is in fact the sequential nature of the standard peripheral devices which causes problems when we consider their connection to the concurrently operating central processing component of a data flow system. This problem is examined in the next chapter.

20

Input output and files

One aspect of programming that is often skimmed over in the discussion of data flow programming systems is, rather surprisingly, that of input and output, particularly when it involves the use of files. One reason for this is that the single-assignment concept used in data flow implies that there is no such thing as a variable. Hence, it is sometimes argued, nothing can change its value once it has been given a value. This argument is applied to files, and it would appear to be impossible to update files!

The other problem with i/o is more applicable to simple data-driven models, which require all their input to be present in order to begin execution. This would seem to make interactive programs (which need to perform some output before accepting all the input) impossible to write.

In this chapter both these problems will be studied, and solutions suggested. Firstly let us consider the problem of input and output. In particular we shall consider the problem of not knowing before execution starts how much input (or output) is going to be required (produced).

Any program may be considered to be a mapping from a number of inputs to a number of outputs. In our model we saw that everything could be expressed in terms of the binary domain B. We may express n input values as the product $B \times B \times B \times B \ldots \times B$ (n times). This may be abbreviated as B^n. Any program can therefore be considered to have, say, n inputs and m outputs, and can thus be expressed as a mapping $B^n \rightarrow B^m$ where n and m may be initially undetermined (run-time dependent).

We now introduce some definitions:

When n (m) is determined prior to program execution (i.e. when the program is defined) the program is said to have **fixed size input (output)**.

When n (m) is determinable prior to program execution the program is said to have **predeterminable size input (output)**.

Otherwise a program is said to have **undetermined size input (output)**.

A program with predeterminable size input (output) can readily be transformed into one with fixed size input (output) merely by specifying an additional input of fixed size, assuming n (m) to be finite, and bounded.

Although a program with undetermined size output may be less easy to deal with than a program with fixed size or predeterminable size output it is possible to specify it since the output set may be recursively defined. We cannot, however, conveniently represent a program with undetermined size input using the model described so far.

The mechanism of definition by cases allows the programmer to specify the possible domains of separate input parameters. An additional mechanism of definition by composition is required in which a parameter (of unbounded size) can be defined by defining its composition.

For example, if the input required was a set of integers (i.e. elements of INT) terminated by an asterisk (*), then the input parameter domain would be expressed:

$$input : (INT^n \times \{*\}).$$

The actual value of n is determined at run-time by the actual input data. It may, theoretically, be countably infinite. In order to avoid the need to represent infinity only a limited number of input values may be regarded as being accessible at any one time. Eventually earlier input values will become inaccessible unless retained explicitly in the program.

Input can naturally be regarded as a function:

$$\{ 1....n+1 \} \rightarrow INT \cup \{*\}$$
$$input = [a : \{x \mid x <= n\}] \text{ 'an element of INT'},$$
$$input = [a : n+1] *$$

If we wished to access the first entry in a set of n integers we might express the definition of the function as below:

$$\text{func} = [a : INT \times INT^{n-1}] \ a(1)$$

Note that $INT \times INT^{n-1}$ is equivalent to INT^n. The former notation is used to emphasise the fact that $a(1)$ is of type INT.

Input and output

In general we have envisaged input and output as unbounded vectors which need not be constructed, or accessed, in any particular order. Most (if not all) present-day input/output devices are inherently sequential, so there may appear to be a difficulty in mapping a sequence of inputs from, say, a tape drive, to a static input vector, which is how the data flow approach models it. Unbounded i/o may be described using the techniques discussed above.

If random access to large files is required, then some problems may occur in accessing the file serially (as we are forced to do by traditional i/o devices). This problem, however, also exists in control flow languages. All that the data flow approach means is that it is no longer the user's problem, but rather the system programmer's problem, and this is not an unreasonable proposition.

Any practical implementation would probably have to restrict the size of the input or output structure that could be accessed at any time.

The mechanism of definition by composition outlined above enables the programmer to describe input and output. An alternative method was proposed in the original description of Cajole [HOS78]. It was suggested that two functions (head and tail) be defined which delivered, or removed, an item of a given type from a given structure (i.e. the functions required two parameters: a type and a structure). A programmer may find these constructs easier to use, but they can be defined in terms of definition by composition for specific types.

$$\text{e.g. inthead} = [struct : INT \times U] \ struct(1)$$

Streams

The possibility of including streams in our basic data flow model was considered in Chapter 14 when we discussed implementation strategies. Weng discusses the possibility of adding streams to Dennis's basic model in his report [Wen75]. He suggests that streams of tokens be allowed to flow along arcs in a data flow graph. In order to control these streams additional start of stream tokens are required. End of stream tokens are only required if the number of items in a stream is unknown when the first entries in the stream are used. This is often the case as far as input and output are concerned.

There is no denying that many people may feel happier working with a conceptual model that uses streams rather than with the model used in this book which uses only functions and recursion. However, any model that uses streams is likely to require recursive functions anyway. Therefore we have adopted the stream-less model as it is in some sense simpler in that it contains one less construct. We saw in Chapter 14 that streams appeared to be unnecessary and the author believes that both models are equivalent — though there is no proof of this.

21

A program design environment

In the previous chapter we discussed what was meant by an operating system in data flow terms. In this chapter we shall discuss how a data flow programming language might be used to interact with such a system, and how programs might be developed.

The standard operators, and functions, along with the standard types and constants which are provided by a system would form a basic data flow environment. This basic environment could be extended in various ways depending on the mode of use of the system.

Simple interactive use
In the language we have developed a definition such as 'a = b+c', consists of three basic components:

the left-hand side — a variable to which a value is assigned (a);
the assignment symbol (=);
the right-hand side — an expression which may be evaluated (b+c).

As with languages such as APL and Basic it is possible to envisage a system in which expressions that are input directly from the terminal could be evaluated immediately. By inputting definitions names are added to the basic environment. These names can then be referred to in any other expression that is used.

Simple batch use

A set of definitions, and at most one expression may be regarded as a program. It would be possible to allow access to files by using an expression such as:

$$\text{FILE.} \langle \text{name of file} \rangle$$

This would be regarded as the name of a function. To write to a file this function would be referred to on the left-hand side of a definition. To read from a file it would be referred to on the right-hand side.

Other standard i/o functions such as LINEPRINTER, and TAPE-DRIVE could be defined. A terminal could be represented by two functions, CONSOLE.IN, and CONSOLE.OUT. In batch mode CONSOLE.IN would be assigned to the source file to access data which would be placed after the program, and CONSOLE.OUT could be assigned to the default output device. If the default output device was the lineprinter then any output to LINEPRINTER could be printed after any output to CONSOLE.OUT. (A right-hand side expression, used without any left-hand side, would be equivalent to an assignment to CONSOLE.OUT.)

Since files are defined as functions they may be supplied with parameters. Thus CARDREADER(2) would refer to the second object read from the cardreader.

This method of accessing files etc. could also be used in interactive mode.

Saving environments

In order to make the best use of the concept of environments it would be necessary to develop some way of manipulating them. The current environment could be saved in both interactive, and batch mode by assigning it to a name. To allow for this form of assignment we would need to define a method of typing on the left-hand side. We would also need to introduce a type ENV or 'environment'. A system name such as CURRENT could refer to the current environment; thus to save the current environment with the name JOHN1 we would use an assignment such as:

$$\text{JOHN1 : ENV = CURRENT}$$

The basic environment would not be saved, since this would waste space.

Saved environments could be recalled by assigning them to the CURRENT environment. A special operator represented say by + would have to be defined to add a saved environment to another one.

Note that this would involve breaking the single-assignment rule. We are only suggesting that this be done with objects of type ENV.

To recall the environment JOHN1 an assignment such as the one below would be used:

$$CURRENT = + JOHN1$$

Writing a right-hand side alone, without a left-hand side, could be used to do the same thing:

$$+ JOHN1$$

The standard environment could be given a special name such as BASIC. Then to clear the current environment and have just the standard one available as assignment such as CURRENT = BASIC (or just the imperative BASIC) could be used.

It would be possible to remove named environments from the current environment (but not deleted from the store) by using an operator such as −, which would be the opposite of the + operator. Thus to remove the environment JOHN1 from the current environment we would write:

$$CURRENT = - JOHN1 \quad \text{or just} \quad - JOHN1$$

As well as the CURRENT environment, it would also be possible to define a STORE environment which consisted of all named environments (each user would have his own CURRENT and STORE environments; the system could also have a STORE environment which could be accessed by users). To remove an environment from the STORE environment an 'assignment' such as the following could be used:

$$STORE = - JOHN1$$

In an extended system it is possible to envisage assignments being made between users' STORE environments. For example, if there were two users, HUGH and JOHN, it might be possible to assign an environment created by JOHN named NEWJOHN to HUGH's STORE environment by making the assignment:

$$HUGH.FROMJOHN = JOHN.NEWJOHN$$

and HUGH would now know that environment by the name FROMJOHN.

Another way of using environments would be as temporary environments. These environments would be used in only parts of a program. Such an environment would be used as part of the current environment in the evaluation of a program by including it in a

WITH..WEND clause at the appropriate point in the program. This could be done by writing the name of the environment as a definition in a WITH..WEND clause.

Any environment could be amended by using assignments of the form:

$$\langle name \rangle \ = \ + \ (\langle deflist \rangle)$$

An assignment such as: $\langle name \rangle$: ENV = $(\langle deflist \rangle)$ would be an alternative way of creating environments.

Error messages etc.

In order to handle error conditions two types of message could be generated by the system: error messages, and warning messages. In batch mode, evaluation would terminate when an error message was generated, but would continue when a warning message was produced. By termination we mean that no attempt would be made to use the value which should have been delivered by the operation that generated the error condition. Evaluation in all other parts of the program could continue until nothing else could be evaluated. In interactive mode the concept of suspending evaluation would be more useful. The user would then be able to choose whether or not to let the evaluation to continue. Another form of system 'variable' might be defined, namely the STATE. STATE would be a function to which different, extra cases could be added. For instance if the definition such as STATE = [x: WARNING] SUSPEND was made, this would mean that whenever a warning message was generated the function STATE would be executed and evaluation would be SUSPENDed. Possible parameter types for STATE could be: WARNING, and ERROR. Each WARNING and ERROR message could have an integer value associated with it so that by using the function STATE the programmer might write his own error-handling routines. A possible extension would be to define the type INTERRUPT, which would allow the programmer to write some interrupt handlers in data flow.

When evaluation was suspended it might be useful if the current environment could be interrogated as if the program had not been started. The environment could then be altered by adding definitions, adding environments, amending environments etc. Clearly though, it would be undesirable to allow suspended functions to be deleted. After interrogation the user would be allowed to either ask for evaluation to be continued, by redefining STATE by:

$$STATE \ = \ [x : LAST] \ CONTINUE,$$

or abandon evaluation by defining:

$$STATE = [x : LAST] \; ABANDON$$

The values ABANDON, and CONTINUE would have the obvious meaning. In the above examples the type LAST is used to mean the last parameter passed to the function STATE. This would always be the current parameter of STATE, and therefore by defining a function case with this parameter type immediate execution would be obtained.

No program development system would be complete without some form of debugging aids. As an example of the sorts of facilities that could be made available in a data flow environment we will consider two possibilities.

(1) KEEP : By typing KEEP⟨name⟩(⟨list of names⟩) after a WEND all the values of the named functions could be kept available for access outside the scope of that qualification clause. The name given after KEEP would be prefixed to all the kept names; for example, if the name one was kept by writing

$$KEEP \; temp \; (one)$$

it could be referred to by writing temp\one.

(2) LIST : By typing LIST(⟨list of names⟩) after a WEND all the values of the named functions could be printed out when the expression to which the qualification clause is bound was evaluated.

In this chapter we have given some examples of the constructs that could be used in a data flow program design environment. This was done in order to illustrate the types of features that could be made available. In the absence of any complete implementation such a discussion must remain hypothetical, but this chapter should have served to show that an acceptable program design environment, consistent with the data flow model, could be developed.

22

Data flow programming systems: summary

There are two main reasons why, in some sections, this last part of the book may have seemed rather vague. Firstly in the absence of any complete multi-user data flow computing system, no complete operating system has been developed. All the data flow machines built or simulated to date have been single-user systems, and have usually used or assumed the existence of an interface processor to control the interaction with the real world. Thus the problems of controlling complete data flow systems remains an area for development.

Some theoretical studies have been done on what facilities are likely to be required in a data flow programming language in order to write operating systems; an example of this is the proposed resource manager facility of Id mentioned in Chapter 19.

The second reason for the vagueness of some sections is the author's own personal doubts as to the meaning of a data flow operating system. One thing it certainly is not is a conventional operating system for conventional machines rewritten in a data flow language. Some of the functions of an operating system are likely to be built into the way in which a data flow computer executes programs or tasks. Just as we avoided the term 'compiler' in the discussions on the implementation of a data flow programming language, a data flow processor is likely to be a rather different type of computer to the conventional von Neumann machine so that the use of the term 'operating system' might be slightly misleading. The use of such a term leads people to make various assumptions about its function. It is not at all clear at the moment which of these would still be required in a data flow operating system, and which arise from the use of von Neumann architectures, and control flow languages.

The author also believes that if we are to realise the full potential of data flow we shall have to re-examine the nature of the peripheral devices that are currently in use. The sequential nature of the von Neumann machine in which data is passed between components in the architecture has led to the development of sequential peripheral devices. Even random-access devices are inherently sequential and return a stream of values. It is perhaps time to consider the possibilities for parallel access devices; or perhaps we should integrate the processing aspect of computers with the memory, so that all processing is done *in situ*. Mago's reduction machine may be seen to be doing this in a rather limited fashion. This rather futuristic concept is well beyond the scope of the current text, however, and we shall all have to await future developments.

Epilogue: A brief survey of related work

In this book an attempt has been made to introduce the reader to the basic concepts of data flow computing. In doing so various topics have been discussed, for example models of computing, language design, and architecture design. No attempt has been made to cover all aspects of current research into data flow computing in detail. To round off the book we will present a quick tour of some of the teams who were undertaking, or had undertaken, some research in the data flow area at the time of writing (Summer 1984). This survey is not exhaustive, and to those whose work is not included, I apologise, but hope that they will accept the survey as representative.

USA groups
The major group in America is that led by Jack Dennis at MIT, and many of the other groups in the USA have used the MIT work as a basis. Jack Dennis's group are currently partially funded by the Lawrence Livermore Laboratory, and have built a simple version of their data flow machine (see [DMi74], [DLM77], and [DeJ79]). Work is also in progress in the field of programming language design [ADe79], and in application areas. Kosinski has also worked at MIT looking into the formal semantics of data flow programming languages [Kos75].

Another large data flow research project in America was the one at the University of California at Irvine (see [AGo78] and [AGP78]).

They originally took Dennis's graphical notation as a base language, and designed a high-level language which could be compiled into the MIT notation. Since then they have made many changes to the base language — adding and deleting features to fit more closely the view of data flow that they developed — so that it is now significantly different to Dennis's. Various designs for machine architectures have been produced, and work has been done on simulating them. As far as I am aware there is as yet no intention to build an actual machine. Around 1980 both the main researchers, Arvind and Gostelow, left Irvine, but the project is continuing on a smaller scale with Lubomir Bic being the main faculty member involved. Arvind moved to MIT, and is pursuing his research separately from Jack Dennis there, though obviously there is some interaction between the groups. A report on Arvind's ideas for a data flow computer was given in a paper by Arvind and Kathail in 1981 [AKa81].

A research group at the University of Southwestern Louisiana has been doing research into the applications of data flow (including operating systems programming, and automatic programming). A report on some aspects of their work was published in 1979 [SLa79]. They have, to a large extent, based their work on the MIT model.

Other researchers who have been working in close contact with MIT include Milos Ercegovac at the University of California (Los Angeles) (see [Mis79]), and Art Oldehoeft [Old79] and Roy Zingg at Iowa State.

Two groups in the USA are working on major projects not connected with MIT; these are the two groups at Utah. One of them, led by Al Davis, has been working on a data-driven recursive machine [Dav78]; the other is the group consisting of Bob Keller, Gary Lindstrom, and Suhas Patil who are working on a tree-structured parallel demand-driven implementation of Lisp [PKL78]. Neither of these groups have started with data flow as a basis but their work is closely related.

There have been a number of other groups in America who have worked on data flow related projects. The ones listed below reported on their research at a Data Flow Workshop held at MIT in 1979 [Mis79].

W. Cote and R. Ricelli (Wayne State): Cote and Ricelli have designed an architecture to execute basic data flow programs built out of 'standard' devices.

D. Klappholz (Columbia): The Columbia Homogeneous Parallel Processor (CHoPP) is an alternative approach to parallel processing, not based on data flow but useful as a comparison.

Bob Meyer (Clarkson): Bob reported on some work he had done on the application of data flow to image processing, automated cartography, and scene analysis.

K. Otterstein (Purdue): The Purdue group had been studying translation techniques and looked at data flow graphs as an intermediate language. They related data flow graphs to the directed acyclic graphs that may be used to analyse a conventional program. Their work was therefore more closely related to traditional data flow analysis (see, for example, [FOs76]) rather than the model presented in this book.

D. Schwabe (University of California: Los Angeles): A group of researchers led by Gerald Estrin have been developing software to support systems design (SARA — Systems Architecture Apprentice), and Daniel Schwabe has proposed that SARA be used to design data flow architectures.

Earl Schweppe and Elisabeth Unger (Kansas): Earl and Elisabeth have developed a high-level language with elegant mathematical semantics, that uses guarded expressions as the primitive from which all other constructs are built [USc78].

British groups

There are five main centres of data flow research in the UK (East Anglia, Manchester, London (Westfield College), Swansea, and Newcastle). They are in close contact under the auspices of the SERC Distributed Computing Panel. Phil Treleaven became interested in data flow whilst he was at Manchester [GTr76]. He has since moved to Newcastle, and is now more interested in a general approach combining both control flow and data flow ideas [Tre78], [TJo78], [THo80].

Back at Manchester, John Gurd and Ian Watson have designed, and by 1983 had successfully built, one layer of a ring-based data flow machine. The design of this computer was presented in [GWa80]. A high-level language has also been designed [Gla78]. It is probably fair to say that they believe the data flow notation that they have is adequate, rather than ideal, and that their main interest is in machine design.

Ronan Sleep at East Anglia was originally funded to do a comparative study of data flow machine languages, but since about 1980 he has been working on what he terms zero-assignment languages [SBu80].

At Westfield College, London, research was directed at the design and implementation of a high-level textual data flow programming language [HOS78]. The notation presented in this book is most strongly influenced by this work as the author was a member of this team until 1979. Work here could now be considered to be more in the field of functional programming. It is to be hoped that this work will continue when the department moves to King's College as part of the reorganisation of the University of London in 1984.

The author's work at Swansea is probably best represented by the model and language ideas presented in this book which is based on his thesis [Sha82]. A current area of interest is the analysis of parallelism in data flow programs, including a study of how different evaluation strategies influence the utilisation of resources when maximum parallel processing is the desired aim. An early report on this work was given at the Toulouse Data Flow Workshop [Sha79].

Other groups
There are two other major groups that deserve a mention. Firstly there has been some work done in Russia. They have looked at recursive machines [Glu74], and also at a language based on guarded expressions (trigger functions) [Kot79] which resembles in many ways the work of Elisabeth Unger [USc78]. The other main group is the Système LAU group based at Toulouse in France. It could be argued that they are not in fact a data flow group since their motivation was the implementation of a single-assignment language. Their machine is almost in a workable state and various reports have been written ([Com76], [Tou79], [CHS80]). They have already begun to think about their next machine design, and the indications are that they feel that the control overheads are too great for the exploitation of parallelism at the instruction level, and that their new machine will be at a higher level. This is in some senses a retrograde step when we consider the aims of data flow.

Also in France there is a group working at Lille that has been studying a block-based data flow system [Lec79].

For completeness it is probably worth mentioning the work of Ashcroft and Wadge [AWa77] (whose language, Lucid, is a single-assignment language which has often been compared with data flow languages), Kahn [Kah74] (whose work falls within the definition of data flow but would be more appropriately considered as an adaptation of communicating sequential processes [Hoa78]), and the work of the group at IBM on the Business Definition Language [Gol75], which, like Jackson [Jac75] and Yourdon [You75], uses data flow principles in the design of programs.

References

[Ada70] D. A. Adams, A model for parallel computations, in *Parallel Processor Systems, Technologies, and Applications*, L. C. Hobbs *et al.* (Ed.), Spartan, 1970, pp. 311–333.

[ADe79] W. B. Ackerman, J. B. Dennis, VAL — A value-oriented algorithmic language: Preliminary reference manual, MIT Laboratory for Computer Science Technical Report 218, June 1979.

[AGo78] Arvind, K. P. Gostelow, Data flow computer architecture: Research and Goals, Technical Report No. 113, Dept. of Information and Computer Science, University of California, Irvine, February 1978.

[AGP78] Arvind, K. P. Gostelow, W. Plouffe, An asynochronous programming language and computing machine, Technical Report No. 114a, Dept. of Information and Computer Science, University of California, Irvine, December 1978 (revised June 1980).

[AKa81] Arvind, V. Kathail, A multiple processor data flow machine that supports generalised procedures, 8th Annual Symposium on Computer Architecture, *Computer Architecture News*, 9, 3, May 1981, 291–302.

[And65] J. P. Anderson, Program structures for parallel processing, *Comm. of the ACM*, 8, 12, December 1965, 786–788.

[AWa77] E. A. Ashcroft, W. W. Wadge, Lucid: a nonprocedural language with iteration, *Comm. of the ACM*, 20, 7, July 1977, 519–526.

[Bac78] J. Backus, Can programming be liberated from the von Neumann style? A functional style and its algebra of programs, 1977 ACM Turing Award Lecture, *Comm. of the ACM*, 21, 8, August 1978, 613–641.

[Bau76] F. L. Bauer, Variables considered harmful, in *Language Hierarchies, and Interfaces*, F. L. Bauer (Ed.), Springer-Verlag Lecture Notes in Computer Science No. 46, 1976, pp. 230–241.

[BDa77] R. M. Burstall, J. Darlington, A transformation system for developing recursive programs, *Journal of the ACM*, **24**, 7, January 1977, 44–67.

[Bir76] R. Bird, *Programs and Machines: An Introduction to the Theory of Computation*, Wiley, 1976.

[Bir80] R. Bird, Tabulation techniques for recursive programs, *ACM Computing Surveys*, **12**, 4, December 1980, 403–417.

[BJa66] C. Bohm, G. Jacoponi, Flow diagrams, Turing machines, and languages with only two formation rules, *Comm. of the ACM*, **9**, 5, May 1966, 366–371.

[Bur75] W. H. Burge, *Recursive Programming Techniques*, Addison-Wesley, 1975.

[Cha71] D. D. Chamberlin, The single-assignment approach to parallel processing, *AFIPS, Fall Joint Computer Conference*, **39**, 1971, 263–269.

[CHS80] D. Comte, N. Hifdi, J. C. Syre, The data drive LAU multiprocessor system: Results and perspective, *Information Processing 80*, North-Holland, 1980, pp. 175–180.

[Com76] D. Comte *et al.*, Teau 9/7: Système LAU – summary in English Report no. 11/3059 ONERA CERT-DERI, Toulouse, 1976.

[Dav78] A. L. Davis, The architecture, and system methodology of DDM1: A recursively structured data driven machine, *Proc. of 8th Symposium on Computer Architecture*, 1978, pp. 210–215.

[DDH72] O. J. Dahl, E. Dijkstra, C. A. R. Hoare, *Structured Programming*, Academic Press, 1972.

[DeJ74] J. B. Dennis, First version of a data flow procedure language, Project MAC Technical Memo No. 61, MIT, May 1975; also in Springer-Verlag Lecture Notes in Computer Science No. 19, 1974, pp. 362–376.

[DeJ79] J. B. Dennis, The varieties of data flow computer, 1st International Conference on Distributed Computing Systems, October 1979.

[DeP74] P. J. Denning, Is 'structured programming' any longer the right term?, *ACM Operating Systems Review*, **8**, 4, October 1974, 4–6.

[Dij68] E. Dijkstra, Goto statement considered harmful, Letter to the Editor, *Comm. of the ACM*, **11**, 3, March 1968, pp. 147–148.

[Dij76] E. Dijkstra, Guarded commands, nondeterminancy, and calculus for the derivation of programs, in *Language Hierarchies and Interfaces*, F. L. Bauer (Ed.), Springer-Verlag Lecture Notes in Computer Science No. 46, 1976, pp. 111–124.

[DLM77] J. B. Dennis, D. K. Leung, D. P. Misunas, A highly parallel processor using a data flow machine language, MIT Laboratory for Computer Science, Computation Structures Group Memo 134, June 1977 (revised June 1979).

[DMi74] J. B. Dennis, D. P. Misunas, A preliminary architecture for a basic data flow processor, MIT Laboratory for Computer Science, Computation Structures Group Memo 102, August 1974.

[DRe81] J. Darlington, M. Reeve, ALICE: A multiprocessor reduction machine for the parallel evaluation of applicative languages, *ACM Conference on Functional Programming and Computer Architecture*, October 1981, pp. 65–75.

[FOs76] L. D. Fosdick, L. J. Osterweil, Data flow analysis in software reliability, *ACM Computing Surveys*, **8**, 3, September 1976, 305–330.

[FWi79] D. P. Friedman, D. S. Wise, An approach to fair applicative multiprogramming, *Proceedings of International Symposium on Semantics of Concurrent Computation*, published as Springer-Verlag Lecture Notes in Computer Science No. 70, July 1979, pp. 203–225.

[Gla78] J. Glauert, A single assignment language for data flow computing, M.Sc. Thesis, University of Manchester, January 1978.

[Glu74] V. M. Glushkov *et al.*, Recursive machines and computing technology, *Information Processing '74*, North-Holland, 1974, pp. 65–70.

[Gol75] P. C. Goldberg, Structured programming for non-programmers, IBM Research Report, 1975.

[Gri77] D. Gries, An exercise in proving parallel programs correct, *Comm. of the ACM*, **20**, 12, December 1977, 921–930.

[GTr76] J. Gurd, P. C. Treleaven, A highly parallel computer architecture, University of Manchester Internal Report, April 1976.

[GvN63] H. H. Goldstine, J. von Neumann, On the principles of large computing machines, unpublished paper (1946), included in *John von Neumann: Collected Works*, A. H. Taub (Ed.), Vol. V (*Design of Computers, Theory of Automata and Numerical Analysis*), Pergamon Press, 1963, pp. 1–32.

[GWa80] J. Gurd, I. Watson, Data-driven system for high speed parallel computing Part 2: Hardware design, *Computer Design*, June 1980, 97–106.

[HGl81] C. L. Hankin, H. W. Glaser, The data flow programming language CAJOLE − An informal introduction, *SIGPLAN Notices*, **16**, 7, July 1981, 35−44.

[HKi76] S. L. Hantler, J. C. King, An introduction to proving the correctness of programs, *ACM Computing Surveys,* **8**, 3, September 1976, 331−353.

[HMo76] P. Henderson, J. H. Morris Jr, A lazy evaluator, *ACM Symposium on Principles of Programming Languages*, 1976, pp. 95−103.

[Hoa78] C. A. R. Hoare, Communicating sequential processes, *Comm. of the ACM,* **21**, 8, August 1978, 666−677.

[HOS78] C. L. Hankin, P. E. Osmon, J. A. Sharp, A data flow model of computation, unpublished research proposal, 1978.

[HSh77] C. L. Hankin, J. A. Sharp, An informal introduction to HASAL, internal document, August, 1977.

[Ive62] K. F. Iverson, *A Programming Language*, Wiley, 1962.

[Jac75] M. A. Jackson, *Principles of Program Design*, Academic Press, 1975.

[Kah74] G. Kahn, The semantics of a simple language for parallel processing, *Information Processing '74*, North-Holland, 1974, pp. 471−475.

[Kin67] P. J. H. King, Decision tables, *The Computer Journal*, **10**, 2, August 1967.

[Knu74] D. E. Knuth, Structured programming with 'goto' statements, *ACM Computing Surveys*, **6**, 4, December 1974, 261−301.

[Kor66] R. R. Korfhage, *Logic and Algorithms*, Wiley, 1966, p. 75.

[Kos73] P. R. Kosinski, A data flow programming language, IBM Research Report RC 4264, March 1973.
Also see: A data flow language for operating systems programming, Proc. of the ACM SIGPLAN-SIGOPS Interface meeting, *SIGPLAN Notices*, **8**, 9, September 1973, 89−94.

[Kos75] P. R. Kosinski, Mathematical semantics and data flow programming, MIT Project MAC Computation Structures Group, Memo 135, December 1975. (Also presented at ACM Symposium on Principles of Programming Languages, January 1976.)
Also see: A straightforward denotational semantics for non-determinate data flow programs, MIT Lab for Computer Science Computation Structures Group, Memo 157, December 1977. (Also presented at 5th Annual Symposium on Principles of Programming languages, January 1978).

[Kot79] V. E. Kotov, An integrated trigger function parallel system, presented at 1st European Conference on Parallel and Distributed Computing, Toulouse, February 1979.

[Kow74] R. Kowalski, Predicate logic as a programming language, *Information Processing '74*, North-Holland, 1974, pp. 569–574.

[Lan64] P. J. Landin, The mechanical evaluation of expressions, *The Computer Journal*, 6, 1964, 308–320.

[Lan66] P. J. Landin, The next 700 programming languages, *Comm. of the ACM*, 9, 3, March 1966, 157–166.

[Lec79] M. P. Lecouffe, Traitement dynamique en assignation unique par blocs, presented at Toulouse Data Flow Workshop, February 1979.

[Mag80] G. A. Mago, A cellular computer architecture for functional programming, Digest of papers, IEEE Computer Society COMPCON, Spring 1980, pp. 179–187.

[McC60] J. McCarthy, Recursive functions of symbolic expressions and their computation by machine, *Comm. of the ACM*, 3, 4, April 1960, 184–195.

[Mis78] D. P. Misunas, A computer architecture for data flow computation, Laboratory for Computer Science Technical Memo 100, MIT, March 1978.

[Mis79] D. P. Misunas, Report on the second workshop on data flow computer and program organisation, Laboratory for Computer Science Technical Memo 136, MIT, June 1979.

[Old79] A. E. Oldehoeft, Simulate data flow execution of computer programs, presented at Toulouse Data Flow Workshop, February 1979.

[Par72] D. L. Parnas, On the criteria to be used in decomposing systems into modules, *Comm. of the ACM*, 15, 12, December 1972, 1053–1062.

[Par82] D. Parkinson, Practical parallel processors and their uses, in *Parallel Processing Systems*, D. J. Evans (Ed.), Cambridge University Press, 1982, pp. 215–236.

[PKL78] S. Patil, R. M. Keller, G. Lindstrom, An architecture for a loosely coupled parallel processor (Draft), University of Utah, Report No. UUCS-78-105, July 1978.

[PRe76] L. Presser, G. Rector, A case study in disciplined design, Infotech State of the Art Report on Structured Programming, 1976, pp. 324–334.

[RLe77] L. Robinson, K. N. Levitt, Proof techniques for hierarchically structured programs, *Comm. of the ACM*, 20, 4, April 1977, 271–283.

[Rum77] J. E. Rumbaugh, A data flow multiprocessor, *IEEE Trans. on Computers*, C-26, 2, February 1977, 138–146.
Also see: The parallel asynchronous computer architecture for

data flow programs, Project MAC Technical Report TR 150, MIT, 1975.

[SBu80] R. Sleep, W. Burton, Towards a zero assignment parallel processor, privately circulated report, 1980.

[Sch77] J. Schwartz, Using annotations to make recursion equations behave, University of Edinburgh, Dept. of Artificial Intelligence Research Report 43, September 1977.

[Sch79] R. M. Schell Jr, Methods for constructing parallel compilers for use in a multiprocessor environment, University of Illinois at Urbana-Champaign, Ph.D. Thesis, Report UIUCDCS-R-79-958, February 1979.

[Sha79] J. A. Sharp, The analysis of data flow programs, presented at Toulouse Data Flow Workshop, February 1979.

[Sha80] J. A. Sharp, Some thoughts on data flow architectures, *Computer Architecture News*, **8**, 4, June 1980, 11—21.

[Sha82] J. A. Sharp, The programmer's approach to data flow as a basis for parallel processing, Ph.D. Thesis, University of London, February 1982.

[SLa79] B. D. Shriver, S. P. Landry, An overview of data flow related research at the University of Southwestern Louisiana, presented at Toulouse Data Flow Workshop, February 1979.

[TJo78] P. C. Treleaven, S. B. Jones, Highly concurrent general purpose computing systems, University of Newcastle upon Tyne Computing Laboratory Report SRM/200, April 1978.

[THo80] P. C. Treleaven, R. P. Hopkins, Decentralised computation, University of Newcastle upon Tyne Computing Laboratory Report ARM/20, September 1980.

[Tou79] Système LAU, various reports presented at Toulouse Data Flow Workshop, and at subsequent 1st European Conference on Parallel and Distributed Computing, February 1979.

[Tre78] P. C. Treleaven, Control inadequacies in data flow computation, privately circulated discussion document, March 1978.

[Tur76] D. A. Turner, SASL Language Manual, University of St. Andrews, Report CS/75/1, revised December 1976.
Also see: A new implementation technique for applicative language, *Software — Practice and Experience*, **9**, 1, January 1979, pp. 31—49.

[Tur82] D. A. Turner, Recursion equations as a programming language, in *Functional Programming and its Applications*, J. Darlington *et al.* (Eds.), Cambridge University Press, 1982.

[Tur84] D. A. Turner, Functional programs as executable specifications, presentation at Royal Society discussion meeting on

'Mathematical Logic and Programming Languages', February 1984.

[USc78] E. A. Unger, E. J. Schweppe, A concurrent model: fundamentals, privately circulated, May 1978. Also presented at Toulouse Data Flow Workshop, February 1979.

[Wad78] W. Wadge, Lucid and its dataflow semantics, presentation made at a mini-workshop on 'Data Directed Computation', held at the University of Newcastle upon Tyne, June 1978.

[Wen75] K. S. Weng, Stream oriented computation in recursive data flow schemas, Project MAC Technical Memo 68, MIT, October 1975.

[Wir71] N. Wirth, Program development by stepwise refinement, *Comm. of the ACM,* **14**, 4, April 1971, 221—227.

[Wir77] N. Wirth, MODULA: A programming language for modular multiprogramming, *Software Practice and Experience,* **7**, 1977, 3—35.

[WPP77] D. H. D. Warren, L. M. Pereira, F. Pereira, Prolog — The language and its implementation compared with Lisp, Proceedings of the Symposium on Artificial Intelligence and Programming Languages, *SIGPLAN Notices,* **12**, 8, August 1977, 109—115.

[WSh73] W. Wulf, M. Shaw, Global variables considered harmful, *SIGPLAN Notices,* **7**, 2, February 1973, 28—34.

[You75] E. Yourdon, *Techniques in Program Structure and Design,* Prentice-Hall, 1975.

Index